Everyday Life Lessons
Living Life with Ease and Grace

Patricia Zimmerman

WDC
PUBLISHING CO., INC.
Light always overcomes the darkness

Everyday Life Lessons: Living Life with Ease and Grace

The author of this book does not dispense medical advice or advocate the use of any technique as a form of treatment either directly or indirectly for physical, psychological, or medical problems without the advice of a physician. The intent of the author is only to offer information of a general nature to help you in your quest for emotional and spiritual well-being. In the event you use any of the information in this book for yourself, which is your constitutional right, the author and the publisher assume no responsibility for your actions.

Published and distributed in the United States by WDC Publishing. For information, contact WDC Publishing Co., Inc. at info.wdcpublishing@gmail.com.

Cover design by Mary Beth Wilker, Wilker Design and Marketing
Consultant: Steven Bauer, Hollow Tree Literary Services
ISBN: 978-0-9962475-5-9

Library of Congress Cataloging-in-Publication Data: Not available at time of printing.

Dedication

This book is dedicated to all those who struggle
to find meaning and purpose in life.

We are here to heal, not to harm.
We are here to love, not to hate.
We are here to create, not to destroy.
We are ALL One.
~ Anonymous

Always pray to have
eyes that see the best in people,
a heart that forgives the worst,
a mind that forgets the bad,
and a soul that never loses faith in God.
~ Anonymous

Acknowledgements

My sincerest and deepest gratitude to all those who have loved and supported me on my journey, for without you this book would not have been possible:

- To Source/God and all of the Divine, to whom I dedicate my life and all that I do.
- To my mother, Barbara Markowski, and my husband, Chuck — for your unending love and support, for your faith in me, and for your acceptance of my journey.
- To my children, their spouses, and my grandchildren — for your patience with me as I walk this path. It is not an easy path to walk, but it is truly a most rewarding one!
- To Elliott and Diane Jackson — My life changed when we met, and I will be forever grateful for all you have done and will do for me and for White Dove Circle of Light and Love.
- To my many teachers in Spirit and in the physical — thank you for helping me on my journey. You helped me to remember who I Am and that life does not have to be as difficult or as miserable as we choose to make it.

I love you all so very much! Namaste.

Synopsis

There is a spiritual awakening taking place, and the momentum is building. Can you feel it? People are beginning to wake up, realizing there is more to life than what we have been taught. People are eager to understand life and how it really works. They want to know why mankind suffers and what it will take to change the world. They are searching for answers, and they want Truth.

Life is simple, yet we make it complicated. When you open your mind to expand your knowledge, you begin to look at life from a different perspective—one that makes perfect sense!

Everyday Life Lessons: Living Life with Ease and Grace was written for those who struggle to find meaning and purpose in life. Earth is a school that teaches many lessons. The goal of any student is to graduate. This book will help you to graduate from this school called Earth.

This book will help you better understand the gift of free choice and our journey back to Oneness with God. It explains how you planned your life before coming into physical form and how you create your life with every choice you make. It details a map for success and teaches how to attain and maintain prosperity. It contains tools for health and well-being, for protection, and for spiritual growth.

Life is a gift. Embrace life and all it has to offer.

About the Author

Patricia M. Zimmerman is an ordained minister, spiritual counselor, metaphysical teacher, healing practitioner, author, and founder of White Dove Circle of Light and Love, a spiritual, non-profit organization where one can find true healing for the mind, body, and spirit. She teaches classes on how to live life, looking at the self to bring about change. Her greatest teacher is life itself.

This is her second book. Her first, *Self-Empowerment: The Only Way to Live*, came out in 2015.

Table of Contents

Disclaimer

What I share with you in this book are my truths. If they resonate with you, they will become your truths, too. My truths were learned from the hundreds of spiritual books I've read over a span of thirty-plus years on my quest for Truth. My truths also come from my experiences in life, my experience in past-life regression, and my experience in helping others to heal their lives. Experience is the best teacher there is.

This book was not written to change your beliefs, but to introduce you to another way of thinking and looking at life. One thing I have learned in my quest for Truth is that much of what religion has taught is not Truth.

One of the many lessons we are to learn in life is discernment—to discern that which is Absolute Truth (Source/God's Truth) and that which is our perception of what truth is. To achieve this, we must always keep an open mind. People who refuse to open their minds to the truth are not ready to hear it. Life is fair when you open your mind to Truth.

As John Heywood stated in 1546, "There is none so blind as those who will not see."[1] The most misguided people in the world are those who choose to keep a closed mind.

[19]The judgment of condemnation is this:
the light came into the world,
but men loved darkness rather than light
because their deeds were wicked.
[20]Everyone who practices evil
hates the light;
he does not come near it
for fear his deeds will be exposed.
[21]But he who acts in truth
comes into the light,
to make clear
that his deeds are done in God. (John 3:19-21) [2]

Truth is Truth. God's Truth never changes and needs no defending. If one must build an army to defend one's truth, then one is not working with God's Truth (Absolute Truth). If hearing the Truth angers one, that person's perception of truth is not Truth. Our soul always recognizes that which is Truth. The spirit must seek it. The Truth shall set you free!

Introduction

Why does God allow poverty, famine, war, and other social maladies to exist? Why are some people born into affluence and others born into poverty? Why do some people have plenty of food while others starve? If we all want peace, why do wars exist? It's hard to find meaning and purpose in life as we face life's many challenges.

I was born and raised Catholic as a child, and I aspired to be a nun when I grew up, but during my early religious education, there were many things taught that did not make sense to me. For instance, if God is a loving God, why are we taught to fear God? You cannot love something you fear. Why is God considered masculine and not feminine? Why does Christianity focus more on Jesus than on God? Jesus came here to teach us about the Love of God and to show us the way. He was a great teacher, as was Buddha, Krishna, and many others before him.

When I married my husband, I became Presbyterian, still yearning for answers. Nothing in this religion helped me to better understand life. So I began my own spiritual journey to find Truth—God's Truth, not what others believed to be truth.

The only rule given by our Creator, the Source of our being, was to "Love one another as I have loved you." This means accepting and allowing people to be who they are and where they are on their journey through life. We are all at different levels of vibration and knowledge, just as students going through school. But if we can learn to love everyone and everything in life with all our hearts, life will flow with ease and grace.

Religion has its purpose. It is a way to connect us to God when we are lost, but it is not *the way*. The true path to God is through spirituality, not religion. Prayer and meditation help us to FEEL God's love.

When we've found our way, we become spiritual, not religious. I found my way.

Eventually I found myself walking away from organized religion (Christianity) because it no longer fed my soul. I wanted to know who I was, why was I here in life, what was my purpose, why bad things happen to good people, and so much more. The answers I yearned for could not be found in any religion I researched. It was time to find my own truth, and Truth was what I found.

> *When the student is ready, the teacher will appear. When the student is truly ready, the teacher will disappear. ~ Tao Te Ching[3]*

Just because people are religious does not mean they are spiritual. Spirituality does not come from religion. It comes from the soul. Religion should not be confused with spirituality. Religion is dogma—a set of rules, regulations, and rituals created by man that were supposed to help people to grow spiritually. Due to man's imperfection, religion has become corrupt, political, divisive, and a tool for power struggle.

Spirituality is not theology or ideology. It is simply a way of life, pure and original as given by God. Spirituality is a way to connect us to God, the universe, and each other.

At no point is the spiritual journey complete. At no point does anyone know all there is to know. Knowledge is infinite. We continue to learn, grow, change, and expand, for the soul never dies. Once you complete your book of lessons, you continue learning and growing, expanding on and on, throughout eternity. There is much to learn and experience. The more you learn, the more you learn there is to learn. The spiritual journey is never-ending.

Christians only use one book to find their truth, but there are many, many books that teach the Truth beyond what the Bible teaches. The New Testament of the Bible is only a history book written by different men. Very few of Jesus' teachings are included. Jesus taught to his inner circle and those who would listen many years before he was killed—by man. Where are these teachings?

There are many great books channeled through clear vessels such as A.D.K. Luk, Alice A. Bailey, Aurelia Louise Jones, Edgar Cayce, Elliott Eli Jackson, Geraldine Innocente, and Godfré Ray King, to name a few. Most Christians depend on the Bible and their priest or preacher for their information and refuse to look elsewhere. They have closed minds. Why? Is it because they are afraid to learn that what they once knew as truth may not truly be Absolute Truth?

What I share with you in this book are my truths based on what I have learned thirty-plus years of searching. My library is extensive, with well over a thousand books on sacred teachings and metaphysics (the science of beyond the physical). You know you have found Truth when it appears again and again, in different books with different authors, written at different periods of time. The information may be told from a different perspective, but Truth is still evident because Truth never changes.

What I have learned in my search for Truth is that no religion is greater or less than another. All have meaning and purpose and provide a means to connect with God. All religions believe in and pray to God; God has many different names. All religions teach the basic fundamental of life: "Love one another as I have loved you," but few teach how to love unconditionally. We were made in the image and likeness of God—Love.

> *I Am Love. I was born in Love; I will die in Love.*
> *I AM love for I can be nothing else. I AM caring,*
> *giving, protective, honest, true, stable, grounded,*
> *centered, driving, and determined. I AM in the*
> *image of Source/God, which is love. Therefore, so*
> *Love I Am. ~ Source through Elliott Eli Jackson[4]*

Our knowledge expands from one lifetime to another, a result of lessons learned. At any given time, you are the sum total of all your past experiences. Each lifetime we build on knowledge gained from previous lifetimes.

Let's use mathematics as an example. Before we can understand the advanced classes of trigonometry or calculus, we must first learn the basics. We learn how to read and write numbers and then how to count. From there we learn addition and subtraction, multiplication and division, fractions, algebra, and geometry.

Wisdom is applied knowledge, when what we have learned becomes a part of who we are. We can never appreciate the Light (love) until we have been through the dark (fear). We can never appreciate what we have until we have gone without. We will never appreciate peace until we let go of drama. We learn by having been on both sides of a situation (karma), and then by being an observer.

There is a process to life. Move forward one step at a time. Skip a step, and you will go back to learn the missed lesson. Skipping a step on the journey weakens the foundation, and your foundation must be strong. Each step is important as we move forward on our journey through life.

You can't make a kindergartner do college-level work. You can't make someone do something they are not capable of doing. Everyone moves forward in life based on their vibrational level and knowledge learned.

There is no right, and there is no wrong. There is no good, and there is no bad. There are only experiences from which we learn. Sooner or later, we all learn.

Life is fair when we open our hearts and minds to Love. Life is fair when we choose to live a life based in Light and Love. And life does get easier the more we understand how we created our world, accept responsibility for what we have created, and work to change us.

Life is a gift. Treasure it always.

Lesson 1

There is Free Choice throughout the Universes

To understand the concept of free choice, we must understand there is the freedom to choose Light or darkness, God or not-God, reality or unreality, the Self or the not-self.

Free choice, also known as free will, is an essential element of the universe and of understanding the laws of the universe. Even the electron, the smallest particle of energy, has free choice and has elected to do the will of God.

God is not the Great Puppet Master in the sky. God does not decide when we are born, where we are born, or to whom we are born—we do. God does not decide when we are to die; it is a choice made by the soul. God does not tell us what to do or how to do it. God may guide us in the right direction, but ultimately, we must do the work.

God will not interfere in our lives because God respects His/Her own laws—the law and gift of free choice. Free choice is the freedom to choose Light or darkness (fear). Free choice is the freedom to choose God or that which is not God, to listen to our inner guidance or to listen to the fallen angels. Free choice is the freedom to choose God's Truth or our perception of what truth is.

Free choice is the freedom to live life or to escape it. Free choice is the freedom to love and respect ourselves as God has loved us or to give our power away to others because we do not remember who we are.

Free choice is a gift of unconditional love from God. What we do with this gift of free choice is up to us. It is a choice we make collectively and individually—to follow the Light or to follow the darkness.

The Purpose of Creation

God, the "Great I AM," is the creator, owner, and giver of all life in the universe. God is omnipotent. God's powers, abilities, and consciousness are beyond what any human can comprehend.

The nature of God is to allow evolution to take place in every part of creation; therefore, the purpose of evolution is to expand perfection. Out of love, God gave consciousness to all of life so all could share the joy of God's Creation. Everything created by God has a consciousness, but not everything has a soul.

Anything that changes and moves on its own is considered living: the sun, moon, clouds, lightning, trees, plants, birds, animals, mankind, etc. In other words, every living thing has a soul and should be treated as an equal, for God created all living things equally.

The Creation of Earth

The Earth was not created in six days (six 24-hour periods) as told in the Bible. It was created over billions of years. Scientists estimate the Earth is approximately 4.54 billion years old, give or take 50 million years, based on dating the rocks in its ever-changing crust.[5]

The Earth has been a school to the race of man for longer than man realizes. The BBC News reported in March 2015 that scientists had found a jawbone of what they claim to be the very first humans. This specimen was estimated to be 2.8 million years old.[6]

Earth is a school, a place where lessons are learned. We, as humans, came to be co-creators with God. Creation on the physical plane is more difficult than that on higher realms (etheric). Souls who are able to achieve mastery in the physical realm are able to perform higher tasks on the non-physical or etheric realm.

The Creation of Man

"God created man in his image: in the divine image he created him: male and female he created them." (Genesis 1:27[7]) We were all created in the image of God ~ Love. Everything in life was created out of Love; therefore, we are Love. It is time for us to remember this. Love is the glue that holds everything together.

God is both masculine and feminine. Every species in life has a masculine and a feminine; e.g., humans, animals, plants. We were created in God's image; therefore, God is both masculine and feminine.

Love is both masculine and feminine. The masculine aspect of Love is Light and the wisdom of God, while the feminine aspect of Love is nurturing and compassionate.

To the sons and daughters of God, God gave the ability to co-create with Him/Her. In other words, we are creators. What we create is always with God's help, whether we realize it or not.

Cosmic Law dictates that those things on which we focus our attention and think about most are what we create. In other words, energy follows attention.

We create our world through our thoughts, words, and deeds—individually and collectively. Everything begins with a thought, and our thoughts are validated by our words and actions. When our thoughts are constructive, positivity and love result. When our thoughts are destructive, negativity and fear result.

Man's reason for being is to take ideas of God based in love and planted in our consciousness, mold them into form, and bring them to fruition in the physical world, thereby expanding the borders of God-consciousness. For example, man could not fly a rocket or airplane if he were not first given the idea from God. Peaceful protests take place as a result of an idea that came from God. Ideas for art, music, and song come from God.

The purpose of incarnation is for each soul to continue to evolve in a spiritual sense (over time, to become the virtues of God) and to become master of energy and vibration through conscious control and use of his own creative faculties (thought and feeling).[8]

Mankind's goal is to achieve mastery over energy and vibration and to "graduate" from this school called Earth through ascension (the raising of our vibration into higher realms of being). Once achieved, we are able to perform even greater responsibilities in other realms of existence.

Scientists and researchers today only look to the physical world for answers, but there is more to life than that which is physical. Just because we do not see something does not mean it does not exist. You cannot see electricity, but if you stick your finger in an electrical outlet, you will feel it.

Science and Spirit are one. The two can never be separated. Our outer world (physical) is a reflection of our inner world (spiritual). Until man can understand the world within, he will never understand the world without.

Root Races

A root race is similar to a grade level in school. Like school, there are many classrooms with children in a grade, but they are all part of the same grade level or "wave," as it is known in the spiritual realm.

Earth can be compared to a Montessori school—many different levels of souls using the same school room, Earth. The first three root races "graduated" from Earth thousands of years ago. The next four root races are still on earth at this time. A root race is not considered to be complete until the last soul "graduates" from school.

The First Three Root Races

The first three root races on Earth chose to use their free choice to merge with the Light. Because each person in that root race chose to do only the will of God, they came to Earth but did not experience what has been called the "fall" to the plane of relative good and evil.

All came forth and chose to do only the will of God with full awareness of the consequences of choosing Light (Love) or darkness (fear). They chose the Light, remained in the Light, and returned to the Oneness of God. Later in time, man chose to experience darkness, resulting in what is known as the "fall" of man.

In terms that you understand, the fall took place when the symbolic Adam and Eve left the Garden of Eden due to their own free will, a choice they were willing to make. It was this decision that brought about the change.

The Fourth Root Race and Lucifer's Rebellion

The fallen angel, Lucifer, made a choice to use the tremendous Light of God that had been given to him to enter into competition with the Source of our being, God. It is difficult to understand how such an exalted being, one so close to God that he was called "son of the morning" and "Lucifer" (meaning Light-bearer), could choose to rebel.

The story goes that the archangel Lucifer, known to some today as Satan or the Fallen One, became jealous that God did not require all of creation to worship him.

Lucifer still had great light when this took place. His light was so great that the millions of angels who were in his service also chose to separate from God, for they were accustomed to obedience to their leader.

The Fall of Man

Ambition, pride, and self-centeredness are the mark of the fall. It becomes a self-sufficiency that says: "I don't need God. I can do it myself, without God's help." Most of us are still this way today. We only call on God for help when we get into trouble. Rarely do we call on God for help before starting something.

The fall of man took place thousands of years ago and was the descent of mankind into matter and maya. Maya, in ancient Vedic philosophy, is the illusion of a limited, purely physical and mental reality in which our everyday consciousness has become entangled; a veiling of the true Self.

Why does the Omnipotent God allow man to fall to these lower depths of consciousness? Because God respects His/Her own laws—the law of free choice and the gift of free choice.

The "fall of man" was the result of man's misuse of free choice. Man intentionally stopped listening to his inner guidance. Man chose to experiment with that which was not pure. Man chose to become sense-focused instead of God-focused, desiring to focus on pleasure and self-centeredness instead of purity and love for others.

These individuals, known as the laggards, chose to refuse to go along with the Divine plan. They were under the influence of the fallen angels. They were complacent in their thoughts and feelings, and lagged behind in the natural process of evolution. The laggards were arrogant, rebellious, resistant to progress, stubborn, and resentful toward change. There are still many laggards on Earth today.

The laggards' negativity spread into Earth's atmosphere like smog. It was the beginning of the "mist" the Bible talks about ("but a stream was welling up out of the earth and was watering all the surface of the ground," Gen. 2:6[9]). When the mist first appeared, it was like a wisp of smoke and gradually became a fog (also known as "the veil") as time went on. Man began to feel abandoned by or disconnected from God, a choice man made freely. [10]

Consequences of the Fall

The "fall of man" created changes in man's bodily structure. It became more dense, more physical. The I AM Presence (That spark of God, the Great I Am, that resides within each of us) began to decrease in size and influence and for the first time ever, man experienced FEAR (False Evidence Appearing Real). The denser the body, the more physical man became. For the first time, man experienced what we know as "birth" and "death."

The veil also shut off the visible presence of Divine Beings. Man was left in confusion, groping in the darkness (fear). As a result of man's choice to use energy destructively instead of constructively, man began to acquire karma, and in this way became tied to the wheel of birth and rebirth.

The ultimate goal of mankind is to get off the wheel of birth and rebirth and return to the Oneness of God.[11]

The Effect of the Fallen Angels

There are many fallen angels whose vibrations are low, influencing and leading the children of God. Since the fallen angels, also known as lower vibrational entities, are etheric in nature (no physical body), they do not experience what we call "death."

The fallen angels are everywhere, just as there is pollution in the air. We can't see them, but we can hear their negative thoughts whispered in our heads. People who are sensitive to energy can actually feel when they are on or around them. It is up to us to push them out and keep them away (see Appendix, Tools for Protection).

As a result of our intermingling with the fallen angels, karma was created. There is no greater learning tool than to receive back what was once given out. We cry out as the victim, forgetting that we were once on the other end (in the current or past life). There is no need for revenge with karma in place.

We made the choice to listen to the fallen ones, and we react with gossip, anger, envy, jealousy, revenge, and other low-vibrational responses. No one can make us do anything—not even the fallen angels. It is always our choice to live a life of positivity and love or a life of negativity and fear.

Through choices made by humanity, these fallen angels have led mankind into all types of twisted misrepresentations, instigating corruption in government, in the economy, and in every nation on earth. These fallen angels have led mankind down a path of fear in all areas of life, including religion.

Working through man, the fallen angels have worked to eradicate entire groups of people with their crimes against humanity

Some of the more recent malicious leaders include Adolf Hitler (Germany), Joseph Stalin (Russia), Pol Pot (Cambodia), Mao Zedong (China), Kim Jong-il (North Korea), and Jiang Zemin (China).

For thousands of years, there have been political leaders working to eradicate entire groups of people through some of the most horrific genocides and systematic murders in recorded history, most notably Genghis Khan in the thirteenth century.[12]

The fallen angels have only one goal: to lower the vibrations of the children of God. They are even willing to destroy a planet in order to take with them souls who would choose to give them allegiance.

The fallen angels have set up false forms of government and drawn individuals into their camp. Nazism is a clear example of a government of the fallen ones, of a black magician (a person who uses lies and fear to control the people) in physical form being used to mislead millions of children of God into his camp through the fierceness of the voice, the beating of the drum, the military parades, and the excitement of the concept of a super-race.

Luciferians had already implanted pride in the children of God, and they drew them into this mass hypnosis through the magnetism of pride. This has happened over and over throughout the history of mankind.

Civilizations have risen and fallen as the result of the fallen ones influencing the top echelons of government and by slightly perverting the true philosophy of God. It was a choice mankind made to allow itself to be influenced by the fallen angels.

Working through man, the fallen angels turned the Sacred Flame into a fiery pit for damnation

The Sacred Flame is the sacred fire that burns within the heart of every person. This flame embodies the qualities of love, wisdom, and power that manifest in the heart of God and in the heart of your Higher or Christ Self.

The fallen ones have worked through man to create a false theology, turning this beautiful vision of sacred fire into the doctrine of hellfire and damnation known as Gehenna, or the "fires of hell."

Gehenna, also known as Hades or Hell, is the fiery place where Christianity has taught that the wicked are punished after they die or on Judgment Day. In Truth, Gehenna was a garbage dump in a valley outside the walls of Jerusalem. Its fires were fed to incinerate the refuse and to keep the stench down. Those who were denied a proper burial were dumped here as well.[13]

In Christianity, Gehenna was considered to be the place where the wicked were punished. Hades was the Greek word for Sheol, the abode of the dead, and Hell was the fiery place of eternal damnation.[14]

Realistically, it is impossible for a place called hell to exist. The physical body turns to ash when it is burnt (cremation), and that which is non-physical cannot burn. Therefore, it is impossible for a fiery place called hell to exist.

"Hell" is only the state of mind experienced when we feel disconnected from God, and "heaven" is the state of mind when we feel blissful and connected with God. Heaven and hell exist within us, a result of our actions and, therefore, created by the mind.

Working through man, the fallen angels created the concept of sin

The original meaning of sin was "missing the mark." While visiting Rome on vacation, I learned the word "sinner" came about at a time when the pope ruled Italy, politically as well as religiously.

A lord during the time of Jesus was a wealthy landowner who had power and authority over others, like slaves.[15] Many Catholic popes were lords, not priests. Whenever the pope wanted more money, he would come up with a list of "sins" for which the people would have to pay. This became known as the "sin tax." Those who paid this money were known as "sinners"—this only proving that sins are "man" made.

The fallen ones working through man, in their efforts to control the people, have taught Jesus died to "save us" from our sins. This is not true. Jesus was killed for speaking the Truth—something people still have trouble accepting today. Jesus taught about God's love for all of us. Jesus taught that we are all connected; we cannot hurt another without hurting ourselves. He demonstrated how to love unconditionally by loving and accepting everyone (even those who hurt us). People were not ready to hear this message then, just as many are not ready to hear it now.

We came here to learn from our mistakes. We may have made poor decisions and taken part in things that were not for our highest good, but we have never done anything wrong.

Working through man, the fallen angels turned an ancient sacred symbol into a symbol to represent terror

The swastika is a geometric, sacred symbol used in ancient religions throughout the world. The name comes from Sanskrit, denoting "conducive to well-being or auspicious." The symbol has been used in Native American, Indian, Chinese, Mongolian, and Siberian cultures to denote divinity and spirituality.

In Hinduism, the swastika symbolized the sun, prosperity, and good luck, while counterclockwise, it symbolized the night or tantric aspects of Kali. In Buddhism, it symbolized the auspicious footprints of the Buddha. In Chinese, Japanese, and Korean cultures it also represents the whole of creation. To the Hopi, the swastika symbol denoted either the sun (clockwise) or the earth (counterclockwise).

In the 1930s, under the influence of the fallen ones, the Nazi Party used a turned swastika to become the symbol of the Aryan race, but to Jews and the enemies of Nazi Germany, it became the symbol of racism, antisemitism, and terror. The swastika is still used today as a symbol of white supremacy and intimidation because of its association with Nazism.[16]

Working through man, the fallen angels have made God masculine

The fallen angels made God masculine in their effort to dominate and repress women. Women have been held back for thousands of years. Women have not been treated as equals to men. Women are the true leaders, while men are the protectors.

Working through man, the fallen angels have made God vengeful

Religion has taught we should fear God. Fear is the absence of love. You cannot love something you fear. Like a good parent, God gives us many chances, many lifetimes, to learn our lessons. There is no need to fear God. The gift of "free choice" is an example of God's great love for all of us.

Working through man, the fallen angels have taught Jesus is the only son of God

Christianity teaches Jesus is the only son of God and that because we are not worthy of God's love, we must go through Jesus to get to God. This is not true. Jesus taught we are all sons and daughters of God. In other words, Jesus is not the only son of God. Jesus did not ask to be put up on a pedestal. Man put him there.

Jesus is not Lord. He has no power or authority over us. Because of the law and gift of free choice, no one on Spirit side can or will do anything for us if we do not ask for help—not God, not Jesus, nor any of the Divine. And when we ask, help will come through our own inner guidance and through the words and/or actions of others (who listened to their inner guidance).

Summary

The children of God have absorbed the influences of the fallen ones throughout the ages into the deepest depths of fear, away from the Love and Light of God. Without even realizing it, they have taken in the philosophies of the fallen angels unconsciously—their way of life, their morality, their attention to "the good of life."

God is everything and everyone. God is the beginning and the end. God is all there is, was, and ever shall be. God is Love, and God is Light.

As in a wheel, each one of us is a spoke and God is the hub in the middle that keeps us all moving forward. For the wheel to move forward easily, all of the spokes must be equal. We are all equal. Everyone has his or her own unique gifts and talents. No one is greater or less than another.

Man and the Bible

The word Bible is a translation of the Greek word *biblia*, meaning "books."[17] The first writings of the Bible, the part known as the Old Testament, date back to approximately 800-600 B.C.E., when social and political conditions in ancient Israel flourished. Traditions, stories, and laws of ancestors were gathered and written into manuscripts.

The New Testament in the Bible has its roots during the last half of the first century C.E. The Bible is a collection of writings. Half of these writings were letters to new Christians sent by one man, the Apostle Paul.[18]

The other half of the writings—the gospels—were believed to be written by several apostles of Jesus, while other books were written anonymously; some gospels were written in the first person and some in the second person. Many discrepancies exist throughout the writings, and the teachings can be vastly different. As for the authors of the gospels, Mark was considered to be a companion of Peter, and Luke was the companion of Paul, who was not a disciple.[19]

Roman emperor Caesar Flavius Constantine, known as Constantine the Great, was the first Roman emperor to profess Christianity. While not a priest, Constantine called the Council of Nicea in 325 C.E. to establish the first formal Christian religion, the universal Catholic Church, because he feared disputes within the church would cause disorder within the empire. No universally sanctioned scriptures or Bible existed at this time.[20]

The Council of Nicea declared Jesus was the only son of God and the only access to salvation. The Council decided what was acceptable and what was not when it came to the newly formed religion.

The Council of Hippo sanctioned 27 books for the New Testament in 393 C.E. The Council of Carthage in 397 C.E. also confirmed these same books as "authoritative Scriptures of the Church."[21]

It's not sure who decided the number of gospels in the Bible should be greatly reduced to four—Matthew, Mark, Luke, and John. These gospels were most likely chosen because they viewed Jesus as the Messiah. The other gospels saw him as a teacher, a figure of enlightenment, one who could be followed.[22]

The books of the Old and New Testament were strictly forbidden to be translated into other languages in 1229 C.E. by decree of the Council of Toulouse:

> "We prohibit also that the laity should be permitted to have the books of the Old or New Testament; but we most strictly forbid their having any translation of these books."[23]

The Ruling Council of Tarragona in 1234 C.E. declared no one was to possess the books of the Old and New Testaments, and if they did, they were to be turned over to the local bishop within eight days so they may be burned.

> "No one may possess the books of the Old and New Testaments in the Romance language, and if anyone possesses them he must turn them over to the local bishop within eight days after promulgation of this decree, so that they may be burned..."[24]

Oxford professor and theologian John Wycliffe was the first

person to translate the New Testament into English in 1380 C.E. For this "heresy," he was condemned by Arundel, the Archbishop of Canterbury.

In 1536 C.E., William Tyndale was burned at the stake for translating the Bible into English. Tyndale claimed the Church had forbidden anyone to own or read the Bible in an effort to control and restrict the teachings and to enhance their own power and importance.[25]

The gospels of Peter, Thomas, Mary Magdalene (Mary of Magdala), Judas, Matthaias, Philip, Acts of Andrew, John, etc. provided different views of what actually happened during the time of Jesus and were considered heretical by the emperor and were thus vehemently stamped out. These discarded gospels taught we are all sons and daughters of God and call for a personal connection with God without any intermediary. This did not sit well with the priests. To keep the populace under their control, the council banned Christians from reading these books, and burned and buried them. Over time these books became known as the "lost" gospels.

It is important to remember that man founded Christianity based on what he wanted the people to believe in order to grow their own power and self-importance. Man invoked the Bible while Christianizing Jesus with selective and edited stories they wanted people to read in an effort to control the minds of the people.

The King James Version of the Bible

King James I of England, a Protestant and member of the Church of England, was a religious scholar who had re-translated parts of the Bible to create one universally accepted text.[26] Soon after his coronation, he requested the English Bible be revised because of existing inconsistencies he viewed as "corrupt and not answerable to the truth of the original."[27]

Those who were assigned to write this version of the Bible feared the king's wrath and rewrote the book to appease the king. The revised Bible was published in 1611 and was to be read only by ordained clergy to their congregation. Until the 1900s, church members did not have access to the Bible. Members were told to believe everything taught as true or suffer the fires of hell at the time of death.

The King James version of the Bible was viewed as ornate and overly formal in the early 20th century among many mainstream Protestant churches, so it was changed again; the language was made more ordinary and flat. Since then, church members have turned to more contemporary versions of the Bible, such as the Revised Standard Version (1952), the New International Version (1978), and the New Revised Standard Version (1989). A complete New King James Version was published in 1982, complete with modernized spellings.[28]

Like the telephone game we all played as a child, the further away from the source, the more distorted the information becomes. Each subsequent translation of the Bible holds the ideologies of the translating body/bodies.

The Nag Hammadi Library

The Nag Hammadi library is a collection of thirteen ancient books, called codices, containing over fifty texts, discovered near the town of Nag Hammadi, Egypt, in 1945. The library also contained carefully hidden works by Plato and the great Hermetic philosophers of Egypt, a Zoroastrian text, and an exquisitely beautiful hymn about the goddess Isis.[29]

The gospels were written on papyrus and carefully preserved when originally hidden. Large sections of a few texts were lost due to age and deterioration.

There were six major categories contained in the library: information on creation and salvation; the nature of reality, the soul, and the relationship of the soul to the world; sacred Gnostic theology; writings dealing with primarily the feminine deity and spiritual principle; writings pertaining to the lives and experiences of some of the apostles; the sayings of Jesus, as well as the story of his life.

Included in this library were texts once thought to have been destroyed by the early Christians and Gnostic Gospels such as the Gospel of Thomas, the Gospel of Philip, the Gospel of Mary, and the Gospel of Truth. Each gospel contained a different teaching. Jesus taught most of his life, but very few of his actual teachings are found in the Bible.

The Gospel of Thomas is older than the gospels of Matthew, Mark, Luke, and John. It dates back to the earliest days after Jesus died (40-60 C.E.) and is the only gospel that has the actual sayings of Jesus, without storytelling.

The Gospel of Peter describes what happened in the spiritual realm between Jesus' death and resurrection.

The Gospel of Mary of Magdala proved she was an important disciple, the leader of his disciples, to whom Jesus would turn for advice and wisdom. The Gospel of Mary of Magdala interpreted Jesus' words. It revealed the power struggle in the early church between men and women.

Some of the texts described events in Jesus's life that overlap with the biblical version. They contain information about Jesus that had been lost for 1,600 years. This sent scholars spinning. The gospels in the Nag Hammadi affirmed that Jesus was closer to his women devotees than the men. They also claimed Jesus was a Gnostic, meaning "one who knows."

Christians do not accept that Jesus was a member of the Gnostic community. Gnostics have long been persecuted as heretics. Throughout the Dark Ages, whenever a group of Christians, such as the Cathers, would show any sign of being Gnostic, the pope would send troops in to massacre them. Keep in mind, not all popes were priests; many were lords. To the Gnostics, "Father" meant Supreme Being from the kingdom of Light—not the angry, jealous God Christians preach.

It is interesting to note the Gnostic teachings, believed by many early Christians to have been taught by Jesus, are actually closer to the teachings of early Buddhism. Gnostics did not believe in the resurrection of the physical body on the day of Judgment. Jesus taught that no one is excluded from Divine grace and that we all can find our way back to the Light.

The discovery of the Nag Hammadi library should have been a major force to re-evaluate everything we know about the history of the early Christian church and the nature of Gnostism.

The attributes and teachings are quite different than those found in the Bible today. Some teachings criticize common Christian beliefs, such as the virgin birth and the bodily resurrection. These texts that were found are over 2,000 years old.

Scholars investigating the Nag Hammadi library discovered some of the texts teach about the origins of the human race—teachings very different than that of the Bible. These diverse texts range from gospels and poems to universal myths, magic, and mysticism. If the early Christians were known as Gnostics, why did the early Catholic church view Gnostics as heretics? A heretic was anyone who argued there were other forms of Christian teachings and challenged the church, for which they were expelled and persecuted—all in the name of God.

The question must then be asked: With this newly-discovered information, why do Christian churches not acknowledge and share this information with their church members? Quite possibly it is because the church refuses to recognize that early Christianity was by far more diverse than what we are taught today.

Also, why was it once so important for the Catholic Church to proclaim Mary of Magdala a prostitute when, in fact, she was the leader of Jesus's disciples? It wasn't until recent years the church was forced to rescind this teaching when the truth became very public.

Accuracy of the Bible

The question can then be asked, "Can we count on the accuracy of these writings?" Slang, misspellings, and misinterpretations existed in earlier times as they do today. The Bible has been written and rewritten too many times to count, by too many men, each with his own beliefs and agendas, down through the ages as evidenced by King James in 1604.

Whenever someone disagreed with the church's teachings, they were viewed as heretics and killed for their beliefs. Why? What did the church leaders want to remain hidden so badly they took extreme measures to protect their secret? Truth is eternal; lies fall away with time. The Truth may be kept hidden for a while, but eventually it will resurface to disprove the lies.

Churches have had the opportunity for 2,000 years to set mankind free, yet man has grown into greater bondage. Because of the many translations, the Bible is hardly recognizable, compared to what it was when it was first written. Everything suffers through translation. Human opinions and interpretations are imposed upon the original.

Many modern day researchers are of the opinion that several key elements of the Bible, such as references pertaining to karma and re-embodiment, were changed or entirely removed from the Bible during several conventions of the early Christian church.

How many church leaders have looked beyond the Bible to look for life after life, or to explore the origin of man, or to investigate the claims for ancient continents, such as Atlantis and Lemuria?

Many Christian leaders continue to teach through fear and judgment, hell and damnation. They preach we must love one another, but rarely do they teach how to love each other unconditionally. People are beginning to question what they have been taught. People are waking up and walking away from organized religion in search of Truth.

The Spiritual Path

The spiritual path involves getting in touch with your true self. Walking the path brings harmony and balance. It feeds and nurtures the soul.

The spiritual path is a search for Truth—Absolute Truth. God's Truth never changes, unlike our truth, which is constantly changing based on what we know at the time. It is learning what your truth is and allowing others to live their truth.

The spiritual path is the journey back to Love. It is learning to love and accept people for who they are and where they are on their journey.

Walking the spiritual path is not easy. It means constantly looking at yourself and recognizing all your merits and flaws. It means knowing your weaknesses to make them your strengths. It means recognizing your fears to overcome them. It means being willing to change what you do not like about yourself.

To walk the spiritual path means you cannot blame anyone for what has happened to you. Remember, when you point your finger at someone else, there are four fingers pointing back at you. What you are receiving quite possibly is something you once gave out.

To walk the spiritual path means there is no shame in what you once did or who you once were. We all make mistakes; we learn from our mistakes. The important thing is that we learn. Those who are stuck in shame, blame, and guilt cannot heal. Acceptance is the first step in healing, followed by understanding, and then change.

To walk the spiritual path means questioning everything. It means letting go of self-centeredness and finding your own self-worth. It means becoming God-centered. It takes effort to change, but when we do, life will become more meaningful and peaceful.

To walk the spiritual path means questioning who you think you are and how you live your life. As long as you hang on to the old, you cannot bring in the new. As you change, everyone and everything in your world will change with you. Those who cannot change will fall away; others will come in to take their place.

To walk the spiritual path means constantly monitoring your thoughts, words, actions, and feelings. When there is chaos in your life, there is chaos within you. When there is peace within you, there is peace in your world. Where there is peace, there is love.

To walk the spiritual path means to find joy in life, to look for the best in everyone and the gift in every situation. It means being the observer, not the victim. Each person has his or her own story. Look at the bigger picture. To criticize or judge someone means you are still criticizing or judging yourself for something you did in the past.

To walk the spiritual path means learning to love and accept all others for who they are, not what we imagine or desire them to be.

To walk the spiritual path means remembering we all have lessons to learn. Ample opportunities will be presented to each of us to learn our lessons. How we handle each opportunity will determine whether or not we have learned the lesson.

Walking the spiritual path is more than just prayer and

meditation. To walk the spiritual path means seeing God in every-one you meet and in everything you see. We don't meet people by accident. They are meant to cross our path for a reason.

To walk the spiritual path is remembering who you really are—creator. You create your world and what happens in it.

What matters most when you go Home is not what you've done or achieved in life. What matters most is the person you have become as a result of all your experiences.

Life as We Know It is Changing

Learn to trust the journey, even if you do not understand
it. Sometimes what you never wanted or expected
turns out to be exactly what you need. ~ Anonymous

More and more, people today are beginning to question the mean-ing of life. People are asking: Who am I? Why am I here? What is my purpose in life? Why do bad things happen to good people? They are realizing you don't need to be in a church to feel God's presence, and you don't need an intermediary to talk to God.

People don't always want to hear Truth, but they must. We are moving into an era of Truth where the lies and manipulation we know today, our perception of what truth is, can no longer exist.

Why did we choose to experience darkness (fear)? Because we can't appreciate the light until we've been through the dark. We can't appreciate the good until we've been through the bad. We can't appreciate what we have until we have lost. We can never appreci-ate the Truth until we've been through the untruths.

Very little, if any, of the teachings in most Christian churches today is Truth. For several thousand years, man has placed words in the Bible that weren't supposed to be there. Man has changed the Bible to suit himself. That is why there are parts in the Bible that say women are not equal to men. Man wanted to keep women under and behind him, instead of beside and in front of him.

The Bible was not written by God. The original teachings were inspired by God, but man interpreted the messages to be how he wanted them to read. Man saw a way to control what people think and used fear as his basis.

"Hell" is only found in the minds of man; man created it. "Heaven" is the place we go once our life is over. It is where we are asked about our personal accomplishments and the good we accomplished in life.

When we go Home, we will be asked these questions:

- What good you have done for others?
- What good you have done for yourself?
- Did you create a good path for yourself?
- Were you a materialistic person? Were you a nature person? Were you a sky person?
- In your heart, what did you feel?
- Did you follow your heart, or did you follow your gut?
- How did you work to increase the Light (wisdom, applied knowledge) and Love (nurturing, compassion) of the world?
- Is the world a better place as a result of your being in it?

If our answers are not positive and rooted in love, or if we have unresolved issues, we are sent back to Earth to finish what we did not learn. If the answers are acceptable, we move to the realm next to the angelic realm to see if we can guide someone who is in need of assistance, similar to a guidance counselor.

Never do we move to the angelic realm, nor can we ever. No human is an angel, nor can we ever become one.

We come to life to help people, not to do everything for them. There's an old saying: "When you feed a man a fish, he eats for a day. When you teach a man to fish, he eats for the rest of his life." Help someone when they need it, uplift them, teach them, but do not make them dependent on you. If we cannot help someone while in life, we cannot help anyone from the Other Side.

It is easy to do things for people you love, but it is not so easy to do things for people you don't know and for people with whom you've shared lessons. The greatest growth comes from reaching out to people we don't know and have trouble accepting.

Graduation takes place when we have completed the book of lessons laid out for us. These lessons teach us to become the God virtues and to learn to accept everyone and everything in life as an equal. We are all equal in the eyes of God, for God created us all equally.

No matter how long it takes, sooner or later we all graduate from Earth.

Our Journey Back to the Oneness

People everywhere are searching to find God. God can be found in nature, in others, and within. To know God is to love God. To know God is to see God in everyone and everything in life.

The journey back to the Oneness is the journey of all souls on

Earth. As you move forward in life, which choice will you make? Will you follow the Light through a conscious awareness of every thought, word, and deed? Or will you follow the darkness and continue to live in fear? Victimhood is an illusion. There are no victims in life, only co-creators of circumstances—circumstances that resulted (karma) from choices we made in the current or past life.

Life is what we make of it. Learn your lessons well so they won't have to be repeated.

The Immutable Truth

To know the difference between that which is Divine and that which is not requires discrimination, discretion, and constant alertness against urgings that seek to magnify the outer self (ego). It requires good common sense. Question everything, for if you do not, you can never know Truth.

Jesus, Buddha, Krishna, and all other Master teachers throughout time taught of the immeasurable love God has for us all. These great teachers came to show us the way. Through their example, they taught us how to love. They did not ask or desire to be placed on a pedestal—praised, worshipped, and adored. What are they going to do with it? They don't need it. They have no ego; man does. What they want is for us to do our work, as does God.

Love God. Love all that is Divine. Love life. Love your life. Learn your lessons so you can live life with ease and grace.

Universal and Spiritual Laws

Universal laws are the unwavering and unchanging principles that govern every aspect of the universe and are the means by which our world and the entire universe continues to exist, thrive, and expand.

Spiritual laws are not about right or wrong; they are about cause and effect. Once people begin paying attention to their higher will (to follow spiritual laws), life becomes more joyous and meaningful.

Some important universal and spiritual laws include:

The Law of Divine Oneness: Everyone and everything is connected. Whatever we think, say, do, and believe will have a direct effect on others and the universe around us.

The Law of Free Choice: We are allowed to think, say, do, and desire whatever we want, but it is the mis-use of our choices that gets us into trouble, creating karma.

The Law of Vibration: Everything in the universe moves, vibrates, and travels in circular patterns. Each sound, object, and thought has its own vibrational frequency unique unto itself. The same pattern of vibration applies to our thoughts, feelings, desires, and wills.

The Law of Action: In order to manifest what we desire, we must engage in actions that support our thoughts, dreams, beliefs and emotions.

The Law of Cause and Effect (Karma): Nothing happens by chance. For every action, there is a reaction.

For everything we give out, we will get back. What we reap, we will sow.

The Law of Attraction: Energy is magnetized. We attract to us that which is like us and that which we need to complete our lessons—events, things, and people that come into our lives.

The Law of Polarity: Everything is on a continuum and has an exact opposite. Negative thoughts can be transformed by focusing on positive thoughts.

The Law of Relativity: Everything and everyone in life will receive a series of challenges or lessons for the purpose of strengthening the Light within. Comparing our problems to others' problems is allowed in its proper perspective for us to learn from; therefore, we will always find someone who is worse off than we are.

The Law of Rhythm: Everything vibrates and moves to certain rhythms; i.e., seasons, cycles, stages of development, and behavior patterns.

The Law of Cycles: For every up, there will be an equal down. For every high, there will be a low. For every beginning, there will be an end.

The Law of Gender: All of creation has a masculine and a feminine aspect; therefore, everyone and everything is both male and female. This includes Source/God.

The Law of Reincarnation: An incarnation is when the soul enters a physical body as a spirit. If there are any unresolved issues at the end of a lifetime, the soul is provided with an opportunity to resolve the issues in another lifetime.

The Law of Resistance: What you resist persists. You may be able to fool the unconscious mind, but the conscious mind always knows. (*See Chapter 3, The Three "Selfs"*)

The Law of Reflection: This law allows us to see ourselves in the reflection of others. Everyone and everything in life is a mirror back to you. You may not like what you see, but what you see is Truth. Change you, and the reflection in the mirror will change, too.

The Law of Attachment: Whoever or whatever you are attached to can manipulate and control you. You become a puppet on a string. Cords are formed as a result of unresolved issues. Cut the cord so you can move on.

The Law of Abundance: Abundance and prosperity are our birthright. The only one stopping you from claiming your abundance is you and your fears.

These are just a few of the many universal and spiritual laws. Take time to get to know them. They will help you to better understand life and how it really works.

The God Virtues

Like the universal and spiritual laws, there are many virtues. We have all heard the saying, "patience is a virtue," but how many of us realize patience is a God virtue? If we do not know what the God virtues are, how can we ever become them?

So what is a virtue? A virtue is a habitual and firm disposition to do good; it governs how we treat each other. There are eight main virtues and many that fall under these main eight virtues. All are rooted in love.

According to *The Sapiential Discourses: Universal Wisdom Book II*, "Chapter 4 – The Wonderful Wiccan Way and Other Truths," under "The Eight Virtues" subsection, the eight main virtues are:

Mirth: Be of good cheer and happy heart, compassionate to yourself and your others. Treat yourself with kindness, laugh at yourself, and remember to never to become too serious in allowing the actions of others to affect you in a negative manner.

Reverence: Hold yourself and all others in the highest esteem. Respect yourself and your others. Cherish your body. If you do this, all will be well.

Honor: Have and hold personal integrity in front of yourself and all others. Let your yes mean yes and your no mean no. Do not be wishy-washy or change with the blowing of the wind.

Humility: Be humble because you are all one, made of the same elements from your Mother/Father Earth. You are not greater or lesser than anyone or anything. You are of the earth, and the earth is of you.

Strength: Endure much and accomplish much. You can do so by gaining your strength through prayer and meditation.

Beauty: Beauty is everywhere, and you are beautiful. Know this, feel this, exude this, and project this, and it shall be you in the eyes of all who may glance at your being.

Power: True power brings about positive effect within and with-on your matrix. When you remember your power, you will have a most positive influence on all that you encounter.

Compassion: This sympathetic or empathetic feeling for your others who may be under the influence of lower portions of the universe, thus causing distress and suffering within and with-on your lives, is a high-vibrational reaction. You know not when you may find yourself in a similar situation and need the very compassion that you have given to your others for yourself. Remember![30]

Source/God channeled through Elliott Eli Jackson: There is no such thing as sin, but there are seven mindsets or vices attached to the seven low vibrational or fallen angels. In *The Sapiential Discourses: Universal Wisdom Book III*, "Chapter 4 – The Number Seven," under the "Sevens of the Angelic Ream" subsection, "Seven Low Vibrational Angels," the vices are:

Excessive Lust: WE tell you, all of you are subjected to lust, yet it is when such desire becomes attached to an act or acts that would be harmful to yourself or others, that it is driven by a lower vibrational angel or angels which, in turn, set influences within the mind of man and woman to carry such out.

Gluttony: Excess in eating and drinking. All of you fully understand that when and if you engage in such, you know it is not in your highest good and that it will affect your being. Therefore, it is, yes, from whispered influences from lower portions of US that would you not use your Earth's bounties in moderation.

Greed: All of you know that which you need and that which you don't. And, further, there is nothing low vibrational, as you understand the term, with maintaining some excess. Yet when you really don't need it and it carries no useful purpose, you are only keeping or maintaining such due to lower vibrational influences. Say what you will, yet, your spiritual self knows full well the truth.

Laziness: Of course, WE have informed you over and over in OUR discourses with you that none of you are lazy. And, of course, there is nothing lower vibrational about taking time for yourself. Yet if that time interferes with your progression in life on any level, it is caused by lower vibrational influences.

Wrath: WE explained to you many times you can't judge your others, you know not what you judge. However, WE speak not here of self-defense. Therefore, the carrying out of judgments that harm yourself or your others, or cause the death of one of you is, yes, in fact, fueled by lower angelic portions of US.

Envy: Need WE say much? There is nothing that one of your others has that you cannot obtain, if you but put your mind to such. Therefore, if you desire to have that which your other has acquired, without the hard work and determination necessary to obtain such, you are in fact, yes influenced by lower whispers of the lower angelic.

Pride: If you are or become so prideful as to not be open-minded to what your others have to say, even if it does not resonate with you, you are in fact influenced to do so by the whispers of lower portions of US.[31]

"Now you have attached names, as you have also have to other portions of the angelic realm, to these angels such as **Lucifer**, **Mammon**, **Asmodeus**, **Beelzebub**, **Satan**, and so forth and so on. To US, the names matter not, fore, there is not one but many. What is important for you to understand is that they are real. WE add that there are angelic beings, such as the Incubus and the Succubus, that attach to sexually harmful behaviors that are not in the highest good, as you understand the term, for any of you because they are attached to excess and obsession. Further, these angelic lower ones are attached to any behaviors that are not for the progression of the individual and the whole toward reunification with US. **Let the Hearer Hear.**"[32]

Lesson 2

The Purpose of Life

"The conquering of self is truly greater than were one to conquer many worlds." ~ Edgar Cayce[33]

Earth is a School

Earth is the school of emotions. We are here to learn to master the emotions, not to let the emotions master us.

To master the emotions means to respond instead of react. It does not mean holding onto our emotions. We can here to experience the emotions, not to deny them.

And like any good school, there is a curriculum—lessons to learn. Some lessons are more challenging than others. Some lessons are repeated; that which we resist persists.

Like school, life can be challenging, especially when we get tested. We created these tests before coming into life to measure what we have learned and what we need yet to learn.

Like children learning to walk, we fall down along the way. We make mistakes. If we cannot admit we made a mistake, we cannot learn from it. If we do not learn from our mistakes, we are doomed to repeat them.

The lessons we choose to learn help us to become God-like—strength, perseverance, courage, compassion, patience, forgiveness, purity, humility, faith, trust, hope, gratitude, joyfulness, fortitude, pride, detachment, mercy, peace, power, service, honor, tolerance, truth, wisdom, and love, the greatest of these. Look for the gifts received within every lesson to find the blessing. There is always a blessing.

We don't grow through the good times; we grow through adversity. The good times are there to balance the lessons and complete the experience. As long as you are in life, there will be lessons.

We have many helpers to guide us while in school—the principal, teachers, teacher's aides, the school nurse, office workers, counselors, etc. While in life, we have many helpers to guide us. Some of our guides or helpers are in the physical world and some are in Spirit. Help is always available. All we have to do is ask!

To move through this school called Earth, we are given a vehicle called the physical body. When we go Home at the end of an incarnation, the physical body is shed, but the soul stays intact. The soul never dies.

The soul carries with it every belief, emotion, and experience from every lifetime, and it is held in our energy field. At any given time we are the sum total of all our experiences (past lives included), and we are connected to these emotions and experiences through the cells of our body.

While in school, we sign up to participate in a variety of activities—sports, debate team, newspaper, nurse's aide, office helper, teacher's aide, etc. In life, we sign up to participate in a variety

of things—sports, politics, theater, music, hobbies, and our voca-
tions. We attend school dances, rallies, and other events. While
our playful times enhance our educational experience, they are
not the main reason for school. The main goal for all students is
to graduate.

And when everything has been charted and planned, the veil
of forgetfulness drops and the spirit comes into this world, ready
to experience life and to learn lessons. It will use a vehicle to
maneuver around in, known as the physical body.

Whatever happens to us in life is always the result of a choice
we made somewhere in time. When we accept responsibility for
what we created in the past (past lives included), we begin to
evolve and grow spiritually through awareness, wisdom, and love.

A Spiritual Awakening is Taking Place

There is a spiritual awakening taking place, and the momentum is building. Look around and you can see it everywhere.
People are beginning to stand up for themselves. They are tired
of being repressed, unheard, and violated. People are working
together to bring about change. And that change is Love.

People are realizing we do not have to be in a church to find
God. Less than twenty percent of the population today regularly attends church. This decline has been taking place over the
past thirty to forty years.[34] As a result of declining attendance,
churches have had to change their teachings or risk losing even
more of the congregation. People are beginning to realize what
they have been taught is not necessarily Truth.

God can be found in the hearts of every man, woman, and

child. God is found in nature. God is everywhere and in every-thing. God is Love, and Love is the glue that holds everything together. We would not be here today without God. We were born in Love, and we will die in Love, for God is Love.

Government officials and people in powerful positions throughout America are being exposed for their lies, greed, and self-centeredness. In this age of technology, it's hard to squelch the truth. Fact-checkers are everywhere because people lie more loudly than ever before. Peaceful protests are taking place around the world. People are uniting to say "Enough!" Governments reflect their people. When the people are ready for change, the government will change with them.

For many, the world we live in appears to be spiraling down fast, but it's not really. Look at life from a different perspective to see what's really going on. The vibration of the earth is rising. The ener-gies coming to Earth at this time are so powerful that everything that is not rooted in Truth, or that has been hidden, is coming to the surface to be dealt with, rectified, and healed. Soon no one will be able to lie without getting caught. Won't this be a glorious time!

The Ultimate Goal of Life

We are all connected in the Tapestry of Life; each one of us is a beautiful thread. The tapestry of life eventually ends in going back to the Oneness with God.

All paths lead to the same destination. Always keep an open mind as you move through life. Much of the experience of life is lost when you are close-minded. Life is filled with truths and non-truths. It is up to you to discern which is which.

You can only go as far as your depth of understanding and comprehension will allow. You are the only person keeping you from achieving greater heights. Learn to get out of your own way.

You are the master of your own life and destiny. You evolve as a soul through a series of experiences. With each experience, you work continually to raise your vibration. Lifetime after lifetime, we build on information gained from our experiences. Our interpretation is limited to the level of learning we have achieved.

Honor and respect the path each person walks, for you do not know the path they walk. Only the highly evolved souls and God can see the bigger picture.

The ultimate goal of life is to graduate from school and return to the Oneness; to be one with God through the perfection of the soul. We incarnate to perfect the soul. Once we have achieved the highest level of perfection, there is no reason to incarnate.

Lesson 3

Understanding Life

"Your true essence is light. Light cannot be damaged, altered, or changed. It can change direction, but it will always be light. Matter consists of solid things, density, and darkness. It can be dented, altered, damaged, and changed. In other words, your temporary illusion of the body can appear to be forever wounded. Your truth, your light, is eternally perfect." ~ Anonymous

The Life Plan

People focus on what happens to the soul after death, but rarely do they ask where the soul was prior to birth. The physical body may die, but the soul can never die. It can only evolve through the challenges and lessons of life's many experiences.

There is a difference between a soul and the spirit. The soul is eternal (the record keeper), while the spirit moves from incarnation to incarnation. Another way to explain this would be to use the analogy of a diamond. The diamond itself represents the soul, and each facet of the diamond represents a lifetime or incarnation in which the spirit resides. The more facets on the diamond or incarnations of the soul, the more the soul is able to reflect the Light within.

All lifetimes take place at the same time. Like a good book, the chapter you are reading is the lifetime you are focused on at the time. The soul's evolution in a lifetime is but one part of the whole.

With each incarnation, we chose a personality to help us through life's experiences. You've heard people say, "he has a jolly spirit" or "she is a kind-hearted spirit."

In order to have the experiences necessary for the current life's lessons, the spirit reviews its progress before coming into a lifetime. The spirit (not God) then decides what it desires to learn or experience. We create an outline, or chart, of what we wanted to experience before coming into life.

Before entering life, you chose your parents, your gender, and your sexual orientation. You chose what race, culture, religion, and country you were to be born in. You chose whether you wanted to be rich or poor. You chose what your body would look like, and you chose the talents and creative abilities, careers and hobbies to help you on your journey.

You chose your name and the day you were born. The child's name and date of birth are important. Together they create an energetic road map of the spirit's purpose for coming into life—its personality, its destiny, and much more, like numerology. Parents think they choose a baby's name when, in Truth, they are just "listening" to the incoming spirit. Often you hear parents say when choosing a name, "No, that doesn't sound right."

You designed your physical body—height and weight, shape

and size, facial and bodily features, hair and eye color, birth marks and birth defects, etc.—depending on lessons you wanted to learn. For example, someone who is beautiful in one life may be learning to find the beauty within in another.

The person who chose to be handicapped or to have a disfigured body knew life was going to be challenging. The decision to be handicapped or disfigured is always a family decision on a soul level. A married couple may want to learn to love someone who is different than them.

Family, friends, relatives, and all those who come in contact with this person are learning lessons. Lessons can be about opening your heart to love, learning it's okay to be different, or learning to accept people as they are. They can even be karmic. Our attitude toward the condition will determine our happiness, and it will decide our spiritual growth.

The eyes are the entranceway to the soul. Each person's eyes are unique. No two are alike because we bring with us different experiences and beliefs based on our past lives.

Look at a photograph of a child under the age of 2. Look at the child's eyes and what do you see? Love? Fear? Hesitation? Curiosity? Sadness? Enthusiasm? Much can be learned about the incoming spirit by looking into its eyes.

You chose your family. Dysfunctional family ties are the result of past life situations. You chose that particular family because you wanted another chance to resolve past issues or because of a loving bond you had in a past life to help support and encourage you in the current life.

You chose the time and day of your birth (early, late, or on time) and the circumstances you were born into—peace or war, plenty or famine, wealth or poverty. You chose whether you would stay with your parents or be adopted, whether your parents would be loving or abusive, etc. You knew all this before your spirit came into life, and you chose it anyway because of what you wanted to learn.

You chose what karma you wanted to balance, lessons you wanted to learn, gifts you wanted to enhance, and fears you wanted to conquer. And you chose those you wanted to help you with these experiences. Our energy is magnetized. We draw to us exactly what we need for our soul's growth.

You chose major life experiences and major dis-eases, and you chose how you would handle each one. You chose obstacles and conflicts to overcome. Your reaction to these experiences is what defines the spirit.

You chose your personality—jolly or grumpy, spendthrift or tightwad, dreamer or realist, dependent or independent, over-achiever or underachiever, left-brained or right-brained, bully or peacemaker, religious or spiritual—to help you with lessons you chose to learn.

You chose how many lovers you would have. You chose whether you would meet up with a soul mate and which lover they would come in as. You did not choose to be alone. We were never meant to be alone.

You even chose how and when you will die, whether by illness or accident, in a war or in your sleep. You planned opportunities to leave life and what you would learn should you decide to stay (near-death experiences).

You chose everything about your body and life plan before coming into life. And then the veil between the spirit world and the physical world drops, and you forget everything so you can experience it all. But not everything is immutable. You, as well as others, can change your chart at any time, and these changes can affect the outcome.

What happens in life is the result of choices you made before you came into life and by choices you make while in life.

Pre-Birth Choices

You chose your parents for their DNA. You knew everything about them—their character and integrity, strengths and weaknesses, marriages and divorces, as well as challenges they would experience. You may have chosen them for karma you wanted to balance.

We learn what to do or what not to do from our parents. You knew the type of parents they would be, present or absent, caring or not, and you chose them anyway. You may have even had a hand in getting the two of them together (married or unmarried).

And you knew you would have the choice to abort the life plan if it would cause unnecessary hardship for the mother or because you altered your life plan.

The choice is always yours when to come into life and when to leave it.

Infertility and the Decision Not to Have Children

Past-life regression is a wonderful tool to help with infertility. Women who can't get pregnant may be unconsciously blaming themselves for losing a baby in a past life, something they had no control over.

The first step in healing is acceptance—accepting what happened because you now understand why this took place. Pregnancy takes place almost immediately because the spirit is nearby, waiting to come in. Subsequent pregnancies take place easily because fear has been removed.

Some women may choose not to have children to learn to be independent. For example, a friend of mine, as a young girl, told her mother "she chose not have children in this lifetime." My friend had experienced a dis-ease (polio) in a past life that made her dependent on others. She chose the current lifetime to balance the experience, to become independent.

Some women may not have been good mothers in a past life and chose not to have children in the current life to observe how to be a good mother. The body may have been designed to keep the mother from getting pregnant to fulfill her life lesson.

Someone close to "graduating" from Earth may have chosen not to incur additional karma by not having children in the current life. Children can be a challenge to raise. They invoke many emotions within us, not all of them positive.

There are many different reasons why women cannot conceive, and they are all spiritual.

Abortion, Miscarriages, and Stillborn Babies

To be aborted, miscarried, or to die in the womb are choices made by the incoming spirit. The spirit may only need the experience of being in the womb, perhaps to experience confinement, or the spirit may know the mother is not ready for a child to come in at that time.

A spirit is not created during pregnancy. The spirit already exists. What is being created is the vehicle for the spirit to maneuver through life.

Since the spirit does not fully enter the physical body until the time of birth, the spirit would not be in the body when the fetus was aborted. Production of the physical vehicle may be terminated, but the spirit never dies.

A spirit may choose to enter its mother's body, however briefly, so the mother and all concerned can experience a particular emotion; i.e., loss or grief. Crib deaths and miscarriages result when the incoming spirit changes its mind. Through the death of a child, our hearts can open to love even more.

If the incoming spirit is linked with a particular family and/ or needs a life experience with that family and the mother is not ready, it will wait for a more appropriate time to come in. It can even come in as another family member at a later time, depending on its life plan.

A client of mine never told anyone, not even her parents or her husband, that she'd had an abortion as a teenager. Her unconscious guilt for having had the abortion blocked every opportunity for her to get pregnant. Eventually my client did get pregnant, and when her daughter was around the age of four, she looked up at her mother at lunch and said, "It's okay if you weren't ready for me before, Mommy. I'm here now."

There is no judgment when it comes to abortion. Man judges, not God. If the mother does not honor the spirit's desire to change its mind, the mother will eventually miscarry or the baby will be stillborn. The choice to come into life is always belongs to the spirit, not God.

We can choose to die as an infant, a child, a teenager, or as an adult. When a spirit has experienced all it came to experience, it goes Home. People should focus more on taking care of children already in life that need help instead of the unborn child.

Adopted Children

Adopted children always end up with the parents they are supposed to be with for their spiritual evolution. The birth mother was the vehicle for the child to come through to get to its intended parents. Birth parents are and always will be the true mother and father because the child has their DNA.

Sudden Infant Death Syndrome (SIDS)

Researchers can never understand what causes SIDS because they do not understand the spirit; not everything is physical.

SIDS takes place when the incarnating spirit changes its mind and decides to go Home. The soft spot on a baby's head is where the spirit can enter and leave the body after birth. It comes and goes as it adjusts to having a body and being in life again. An incoming spirit has up to two years to change its mind. Once the spot has closed, the spirit must live the life it has chosen.

Baby boys have a higher rate of SIDS because we paint their bedroom blue and dress them in blue clothes. Blue is the color of Spirit. The spirit is reminded of where it just came. Pure unconditional love exists on the Other Side of the veil. The conditional love we know is no match for unconditional love. The spirit can get homesick, change its mind, and decide to go Home.

Use the color blue sparingly. It is better to use the colors pink (love), green (healing), purple (spiritual devotion), or yellow (happiness and intellect) to welcome a child into life. Surround your baby with lots of love so there will be no desire to go Home.

Physical challenges

Physical challenges, such as being disabled, disfigured, or deformed, are chosen for soul growth. They can be a humbling experience because you are forced to accept yourself for who you really are. Others must also to learn to accept you just as you are.

Physical challenges teach that you are not your physical body. You are the beautiful soul that lives within the body. They teach not to judge anyone, for you know not the path they walk or the lessons they are learning.

Physical challenges teach you to strive for greater heights as you struggle to overcome your limitations instead of allowing others to do everything for you. The karma being balanced by a person with physical challenges can equal ten or more lifetimes when handled positively.

Physical challenges teach you to not take people and life for granted, as you gain an appreciation for the lessons and blessings of life. A special blessing, grace, is received when you draw on your inner strength and use it to help others.

Death

Death can be difficult to understand when one is not on the spiritual path. What we fear most is the unknown—what comes next for the dying person? For us?

Spirits leave the earth plane in many different ways; death can be expected or unexpected. It is much easier to let go of someone who has been sick for a long time. It is much harder to let go of someone who dies unexpectedly. It is even more difficult to let go when there are unresolved issues (shame, blame, and guilt).

A group of people leaving the earth plane together (for example, a plane crash, school shooting, or terrorist attack) chose to die together before incarnating. Their death usually brings about change.

There are as many ways to die as there are reasons for dying. How and when one dies is a personal choice made before incarnating. We also plan several different exit points before entering life.

If someone appears to be lingering in a comatose state prior to death, he or she may be balancing karma or planning their next life. Quite often the loved one who has just crossed over has chosen to incarnate as their grandchild.

Your soul will recognize your loved one by their eyes, their smile, their mannerisms, and their personality. As the child gets a little older, typically around the age of 3, they may even recognize themselves in pictures and point this out to you. Do not dismiss this information. They just came from Spirit side. They would know better than you!

People who die as infants or young children came in with the specific purpose to help loved ones open their hearts to love and to teach love is the only thing that matters. Quite often, parents are too focused on the material world and have forgotten the "world does not revolve around them." If the death of the child makes us bitter, we close our hearts and wallow in self-pity. Look for the gift in every experience. It will help move you through the sadness.

Once our chart has been completed and we have finished everything we wanted to do, we go Home. Death is *always* the soul's choice, never God's. This is especially hard to understand when someone close to us has chosen to go Home unexpectedly.

When someone you love is dying, love them enough to let them go. Allowing a loved one to suffer because of your own personal needs is self-centered. They are where they want to be, and you are left having to adjust to life. It doesn't seem fair. You want to be with your loved one. If you allow life to play itself out, one day down the road you will understand why your loved one left. If you continue you to drown in your misery, you may never understand.

Remember, the life they chose was for their soul growth! If you were a senior in high school getting ready to graduate, would you stay behind because your friends who were juniors or sophomores were still in school? Of course not! You would know that you will see them again one day in the future. Death is not an ending. It is the beginning of a new way of living for everyone involved.

The grieving process takes time. It allows us to experience every occasion without our loved one. Grieving for longer than one year is not natural and can hinder your loved one's next life experience. Cut the cord between you, or you will drain their energy, weaken their spirit, and make their next life more difficult.

Letting a loved one go when it is time will not only help you with your healing, it will help your loved one in their next life, too.

The Spirit Enters in Four Stages

The spirit does not enter the womb at the time of conception. A spirit is not being born; a vehicle is being created. The spirit enters the physical body in four stages.

Birth

The flutter or movement an expectant mother feels is the spirit present in the physical body. During pregnancy, the spirit goes in and out of the womb to get used to the denseness of a physical body. It does not fully enter the physical body until two days before to two days after birth. This is the **first stage**.

We came from Spirit side where we were nothing but pure Light. For a spirit to remain in a crowded, damp, dark place in the body for nine months could be compared to being imprisoned in a crowded, damp, dark cell—an unnecessary step in the soul's evolution.

When there is no movement in the womb, the spirit is not in the womb. It is nearby letting the parents know what it wants for a name and what it will need for its soul's growth.

This is a hard concept for most people to understand since we have not been taught this Truth. But think of manufacturing of a car. If you decide to contract to have a custom-built car to ride around in, would you live in it the entire time it is being produced? No, but you could try it out from time to time to make sure it is what you wanted. Possession takes place when the car is complete.

The spirit was able to maneuver around freely without a body while in the Spirit realm. It will take some time to get used to the heaviness of a physical body once again.

Awareness

The **second stage** takes place when the personality comes in. The baby begins to respond to its loved ones by smiling, cooing, and making faces. It no longer just eats, sleeps, and wets.

It is extremely important for an infant to be talked to and to feel loved. The human touch is a powerful tool to express love. The tissue in our hands is the same as our heart. We send love through the touch of a hand. Like us, babies need to be held and cuddled to feel loved.

Babies are more sensitive than we realize. They feel different levels of energy better than most adults. Babies can sense the difference between the energy of love and that of fear.

Fear to an infant feels like pins and needles. That is why babies cry for no apparent reason when someone full of fear holds them or when they are in a negative environment.

Adolescence

The **third stage** takes place between the ages of 9 and 14 when we get our karmic package, a ball of energy to be dispersed into our energy field. Because we have spent many lifetimes creating karma, we choose to balance karma from three to four lifetimes during an incarnation. Any more than this would be overwhelming and could cause more damage than good.

The arrival of the karmic package explains the hormonal

changes at the time of puberty; something feels different. Teenagers don't know who they are anymore. Unconsciously, they do not like themselves for who they once were or what they once did. This can show up as acne. Scoliosis can also take place during this stage. Remember, not everything is purely physical.

Adulthood

The fourth stage takes place at the age of 21. It is time for the young adult to begin the life lessons it chose to learn.

The Three "Selfs"

Everyone has an unconscious, conscious, and subconscious self. The subconscious self is always present, guiding the soul along its journey. Whether we work from the unconscious or conscious self will determine where we are on our evolutionary journey.

The Child—The Unconscious Self

The unconscious self is similar to a child—we do things without thinking; we react. We are called "children" of God for a reason; we act like children. We whine and cry out when we don't get our way. We only think of ourselves; we are "self" centered.

Most of us work from the unconscious self. The Ascended Masters (master teachers) call this "sleepwalking through life." We see what we want to see, hear what we want to hear, and know what we want to know. We **react** to situations that come up. We are quick to blame, criticize, and judge when things don't go our way, or we internalize what happened through shame and guilt. Most of us move through life on "autopilot."

This only creates more karma, more experiences we will need to balance.

It is time to grow up and become the adult if we want to graduate life.

The Adult—The Conscious Self

The conscious self is similar to an adult—we begin to think before we speak or act. We begin to look at things from a different perspective outside of the self. We become "other" centered. We become aware of the effect our thoughts, words, and actions will have on us and others. We choose our words wisely.

We **respond** rather than react. To respond means to stop, take a deep breath, and look at what is happening from all perspectives for a clearer understanding of what is taking place. It is through awareness we find peace and direction in life.

The Graduate—The Subconscious Self

The subconscious self is your Higher or Christ Self. It knows only goodness and perfection. It is the image and likeness (Light and Love) of the Creator within you. The Higher Self is that little voice in your head (intuition) that guides you on your path.

When Jesus made his ascension, he became Jesus the Christ, meaning he became his Christ Self. He no longer had need of a physical body. Because Christianity did not understand what the Christ Self was, "Jesus the Christ" was shortened to "Jesus Christ." Christianity refers to Jesus as "Christ" without the true understanding of what the Christ is.

When we have learned to love and accept everyone and

everything in life at the level of vibration and level of knowledge they are, we graduate from earth. We make our ascension into the higher realms of being where there is no longer a need for a physical body or to incarnate (unless we so choose). We choose to go back to the Oneness with God, or we choose to go to other places within the universe (realms, planes of existence, planets, star systems, etc.).

Sooner or later the child must grow up to become the adult. Sooner or later we all graduate from Earth. How long it takes is up to you. If you want to graduate from school, you will stop acting like a child and begin working to become the adult.

Soul Contracts

The soul contract is a sacred contract between two people that both parties agree to honor. The contract is made on a soul level for the soul's evolutionary growth. Two souls promise to balance any karmic lessons between them and to support and help each other while learning life's many lessons.

Marriage

Marriage is man-made to ensure accountability. When two people agree to marry, a soul contract is created on a Spirit level. The two souls agree to honor the contract, to cherish each other, and to help each other on their journey together.

Throughout marriage, challenges arise. Oftentimes, your spouse may be a reflection to see what is going on within you. Take time to look for the lesson to be learned. What we don't like about another is usually something we don't like about ourselves.

If a situation keeps happening over and over, ask "What do I need to learn from this?" What do you need to learn about you? In what area do you need to change? Are there boundaries that need to be set?

We all play roles for each other to see what is going on within us. English poet and playwright William Shakespeare stated it best:

"All the world's a stage,
And all the men and women merely players;
They have their exits and their entrances;
And one man in his time plays many parts,
His acts being seven ages."[35]

Don't try to change your partner. It will not work. Change you and your partner will change with you. Life does not get better by chance. It gets better by change.

Parents

Before coming into life, you chose your parents based on what you wanted to learn. We learn from our parents what to do and what not to do.

You brought two people together for your sake. The pregnant teenager and the person who had a one-night-stand listened to the incoming spirit. In the case of pregnancy as a result of rape, it may have been karmic. You do not get to choose your parents when balancing a horrific act. They are chosen for you by Beings of Light on the Other Side before incarnating.

The incoming spirit knows whether or not the two parents will stay together. Never feel you have to stay together for the children's sake. Their spirit wants the very best for all concerned. It knew before it came into life you probably would not stay together, and it chose you anyway.

In the case of adoption, the spirit knew it would grow up with another mother, yet it chose its birth mother anyway based on what it wanted to experience.

The decision to have a child creates a soul contract—a contract that says as parents, you agree to bring this spirit into life. Nothing more. The contract ends there. Parents do not owe their children anything. Anything received after birth is a blessing and a sign of the parent's love for their child.

Divorce

While we should all work to create love in our marriage, sometimes it is just not possible. It takes two people working together to create a successful marriage.

When a couple first gets together, love is bliss. We are infatuated with our partner. We think we are in love, but we are not. True love comes from years of knowing and accepting our partner for who they really are. It comes from doing things together that both parties enjoy. It comes from working together toward a common goal.

The first year of cohabitation or marriage is often the most difficult because the couple must learn to live together. It is one thing to "love" someone, and it's another thing to "live" with someone. It's the living with someone that brings about challenges in the relationship. We see each other at our best and at our worst. We decide how we're going to spend holidays, if and where we'll go on vacation. The "dating" often ends before the end of the first year together. But once a couple's first year of marriage is behind them, their feelings may change drastically.

Add children or the death of a child to the picture, and everything changes again. It will either bring the couple closer together or it will pull them apart. There are always lessons.

Addiction and abuse, verbal or physical, are extremely difficult challenges for any marriage. It can tear the couple apart on many levels, and the emotional trauma is difficult to release.

A job loss, a serious or long-term dis-ease make us question whether or not we want to continue life as it is, or move onto someone or something else.

And when you have done all you can and your spouse no longer "makes your rivers flow," when you have tried everything possible to make your marriage work (including counseling), and there are still problems, then it is time to separate. If space and time during separation do not heal the wounds, then divorce. No one should remain in a marriage where love is not present. These negative emotions create more damage than they do good.

God wants us to be happy. If we are negative or live in fear, this negativity is spread to everyone we meet. It invokes judgment and criticism, hatred and anger, within the couple and those who know them. This negativity serves no one.

When the soul contract is up, let go of the old to bring in the new. There will be another person for you to love. You were never meant to be alone.

When children are involved, remember, you will always be tied to your "other" through them. Never speak poorly of your children's father or mother. Your children chose the two of you to be their parents based on what they wanted to learn. They will learn what to do or what not to do from your example. Teach your children well. Teach them how to love by being an example of love in action.

The "Death" Process

Death is not an ending; it is a beginning. As we come into life, we cry because we know life will not be easy. When we decide to go Home at the end of life, we cry because we will miss our loved ones.

Misunderstood Concepts of Death

Society has many preconceptions about death. It is viewed as morbid, sad, dark, depressing, and even unnecessary. Most people think of death as something to be feared. They view death as a great tragedy and, most importantly, they believe that death is permanent. These thoughts slow our spiritual progress while here on earth.

Many people fear death because they believe that at the moment of death they will cease to exist.

But energy moves in cycles. The end of one cycle is the beginning of another. We are all going to experience death. The more we understand death, the less we need to fear it.

You cannot destroy energy, but you can change its form. The soul is energy. We may shed the physical body, but the soul remains intact, carrying with it all our thoughts, emotions, memories, and experiences. After "death," we no longer experience through the physical body, but through the mind.

To better understand death, compare the physical body to a car. Throughout life, you will have several different cars. You may lose a car due to an accident, or you may choose to upgrade your car to a newer model. Either way, the choice is yours to repair the current car or get a new one.

Likewise, through its journey, your soul will live in different bodies. The soul is eternal. It can never die.

The Moment of Death

Death is merely the process of moving from a physical body to the pure soul essence on the Other Side of the veil. The physical body is shed much like a snake sheds its layer of skin.

The death process is the same for everyone, no matter how quickly or slowly one dies. At the moment of death, the energy of the spirit begins to separate from the physical body. The spirit is connected to the physical body by a silver cord known as the antahkarana. This cord tethers the spirit to the physical body. Once the cord is cut, the spirit is separated from the physical body creating what we call "death."

At this time people begin to separate the words "body" and "spirit," referring to the "remains" as the body. They refer to the spirit in eulogies and prayers, as if somehow they inherently know the separation of these two terms signifies the transition of the spirit into another realm.

As you journey through the tunnel of death (the tunnel of

white light), your life's history will flash before your eyes. You view your entire life, every single moment, from birth to death, in one astounding flash of color, light, and feeling. The body's heat begins to leave; the body turns cold. The spirit leaves the physical body and becomes wholly encased in the immortal soul. The soul is all that remains when the physical body is shed.[36]

The perceptions, ideas, and beliefs of the spirit accompany it to the next stage of its evolution. No matter what someone did or how they behaved in the physical life, any negative aspect of the spirit is stripped away.

The spirit continues to live, now in a different realm or plane of existence. The elements from which the physical body are made are returned to be recycled into earth, whether burial is in the earth, at sea, or through cremation.

The transition time is near when Light Beings you recognize, as well as loved ones who have already crossed over, come to help guide you back Home. This is real, and it does happen.

Look for the Light at the time of death and follow it. This Light is the tunnel back to God. Let your loved one know it is okay for them to leave and that you will be okay without them. Release them so you both can move forward.

Death is only one step on the soul's evolutionary journey.

The Near-Death Experience

Once a soul decides to leave the body, it goes through what is called the "Tunnel of Lives." Here you see beautiful lights in different intensity, shapes, and sizes, and you hear a variety of sounds from harmonic softness, to howling and banging, to the wind blowing and musical strings playing on their blissful journey back Home. Know that there is nothing to fear.

At this junction you can decide to keep going or return to life to assist others. If you return, it is known as a near-death experience. You may remember fragments of what happened, but you will not remember the entire experience.[37]

You decide when you are ready to leave life, when you have accomplished everything you came to do. There are no accidents in life—only synchronicity.

The choice is always ours whether to return to life or go Home.

Disposition of the Body

Visiting a grave prolongs attachment to a loved one who is no longer there. No spirit ever stays in a coffin in a graveyard. The physical body will decay, but the spirit is eternal. Remember your loved one through prayer and positive thoughts, pictures and memories.

Cremation is the best method for disposal of the physical body because of the concept of attachment. Once a body is not physically here, attachment ceases to exist. This is enormously helpful to the spirit who has transitioned to the Other Side.

Cremation is kinder to the earth. The decomposition process takes a very long time and releases toxic substances in the process. It is easier to loosen attachments by releasing the energy of the body through the fires of purification.

Return the ashes to the earth to complete the cycle of healing. Hanging onto a loved one's ashes is an attachment. Keep them for a while if you must, but just as you must let go of the spirit, you must also release the ashes. You will know when the time is right.

The Life Review

Everything we have ever done and said has been recorded. It is holographic in nature, and it is kept in the Library of Souls in the spiritual realm. Each book contains information of all lives lived by the soul throughout eternity. Each lifetime is a different chapter in your book. It includes a detailed account of every experience you have ever had—every thought, word, and deed—in every lifetime. This is where the soul goes to review its progress.

The life review is a learning tool. You review your life and the impact you had on other people. You see the ripple effect of your actions, and each movie frame of the life you lived is a moment in that life. When you speed up the frame of each life moment, you have an entire picture of how your life was lived.

After reviewing the lifetime, the soul decides what it wants to experience next for its growth. There is no judgment ever from anyone on Spirit side, for there is no one harder on you than you. It is you, and only you, who decides the next step in your evolutionary journey.

The Next Step

There are different planes, realms, and levels of existence we can go to after death. As stated in *The Sapiential Discourses: Universal Wisdom Book* III, Chapter 3—"Death – What Really Happens," under "Non-Acceptance During a Lifetime" section:

> *"As WE related in Book II of the Sapiential series, this plane [Conflictus] is for the souls and spirits that were intolerant or adamantly against a grouping, planet,*

form or animal, sea dweller, country and its people,
and any choice of sexual lifestyle unlike its own. Here
the soul or spirit will choose one of the portions of
US/THEM that they did hate and not accept and be
reincarnated as such. It is the way and progression of a
spirit in all universes." [38]

In other words, we choose to reincarnate as the thing or person we hated to balance karma. We must learn to love that which we hated.

As also stated in *The Sapiential Discourses: Universal Wisdom Book* III, Chapter 3—"Death – What Really Happens," under "More Insight on an Aspect of Afterlife" section:

"Further, the only way to return to US the Oneness is to,
in a lifetime, accept everything and everyone as equal
and treat them as such. This is the reason that many
of you have so many lifetimes, because you refuse to
accept essentially yourself. For all of you are the same,
except each of you are in different encasements. If the
aforementioned total acceptance is not obtained during
a lifetime, as you understand that term, another lifetime
will ensue or be experienced by the spirit that was
housed within the previous encasement within another
encasement on your plane of existence or another. The
next lifetime will be either the form of plant, animal,
human encasement or another form or species. Once
more and more of you begin to accept this truth, and

adhere to such in whatever form you may be, additional
lifetimes are not necessary."[39]

To learn more about living life, you may want to read the entire series of books written by All There Is, Was, and Ever Shall Be, Source/God, and channeled through Elliott Eli Jackson.

Reincarnation

Reincarnation is the belief that when an individual dies, he or she is reborn into another body. This idea has existed in various religions for over 3,000 years, and today there are probably more people on earth who believe in reincarnation than those who do not. Souls are reincarnating faster at this time because there are more mothers—the vehicle necessary to bring life into a physical form—than ever before.

We may shed the physical body at death, but the soul never dies and it holds within itself every experience, belief, and emotion from one lifetime to the next. We incarnate to gain experience.

The Veil Drops

As you reincarnate, a veil comes down, and all memory of past lives is hidden, but familiarity with people, places, and things persists. The veil is an energetic boundary between the mortal realm and the immortal realm. It is necessary so that you will have an absolutely new opportunity for experiences as you embark on each new incarnation.

You remember what you need to remember as you work through your lessons or try to come to terms with old ones.

Something you may be going through in your current life may trigger a reaction, or connection, to a previous life. This latent emotion or experience now becomes a part of the current life, consciously or unconsciously.

Death Teaches Us

Compassion for the choices each soul makes is one of the best ways to deal with death. Compassion for yourself and your loved one is a part of your soul's evolution.

Death teaches lessons of love. You may learn to value life, or you may learn how little others value life. You may learn to live life differently, with more awareness, and hopefully, more love.

Death provides lessons of compassion. Understanding all aspects of death enables you to open your heart more to others. The more you learn from the process of death, the more compassionate you become.

Embracing Death

What does it mean to embrace death? It means not clinging to people who are dying and begging them to get better when, in reality, it is you who is afraid. Their soul is ready to go Home, even if you are not ready for them to go.

Embrace love knowing your loved one is no longer suffering. They are feeling the joy of Divine Light and Love.

A person's life, however young or old, is complete at the time of death. Not everyone needs to live 100 years or more. The soul received everything it needed. When death takes place, the soul returns to its real Home.

To embrace death means to come to a peaceful understanding of the process and meaning of life and death. Most people grieve for themselves at the time of a loved one's death. People grieve for what once was and for what will be. People also grieve because of unresolved issues that show up as blame, shame, and guilt.

Resolve all issues with loved ones before their death so you won't have to recreate the situation in another life for it to be resolved.

Cut the Etheric Cord!

Honor their memory, but do not hang on to your loved one. Incessant crying over what once was will keep you "stuck," and it will drain their energy in the next life. Be grateful for the time you shared. Life is not over because your loved one went on without you.

A good way to release your loved one is to write a letter to him or her, telling this person how much he or she meant to you and how much you loved him or her. End your letter with "I love you, and I release you." Then burn the letter, symbolic of purification, and return the ashes to the earth.

The Triangle of Life

Three is a spiritual number, and everything spiritual comes in threes. And so we, too, experience life in a series of three in order to more fully understand the experiences of life.

We came into life to experience emotions, and that means experiencing all sides of a given situation—what I call the perpetrator, the victim, and the observer. There is something to learn from each role, as each one has a different set of emotions to be experienced.

Visualize an equilateral triangle. The straight line connecting the two bottom angles represents the balance of life (karma), similar to a teeter-totter. Balance is the key to life. Without balance, we flounder when trying to find meaning and purpose.

The bottom angles represent the perpetrator and the victim. The top angle is what I call the observer. From this vantage point both sides can be viewed.

Over our different lifetimes, and sometimes within the same life, we experience playing the roles of perpetrator, victim, and observer in a situation. Let's use the following example:

> **The Perpetrator:** In this role you may kill someone intentionally or unintentionally. There are a myriad of reasons why perpetrators do what they do. They have their own set of emotions and beliefs. What led them to become a perpetrator may have been painful.
>
> **The Victim:** In this role you experience what you once gave out (karma), painful as it may be. Victims have their own set of emotions and beliefs, and their experience can be painful, too. They do not understand why something happened.
>
> **The Observer:** In this role you will know somebody who was killed. Your heart goes out to the family. You experience compassion because you know what it's like to be in that person's shoes; you have been there before. Compassion is heartfelt; empathy is not.

Tears shed help to heal both you and the victim as you open your heart even more to love. You may get a better understanding of the perpetrator and what brought him or her to commit this act of violence. You are able to see and understand both sides now.

There is something to be gained from playing all roles, and this is called LOVE.

The first step in growing love is COMPASSION. It is impossible to have compassion for someone else unless you first experienced a similar situation (past or present life).

The next step to grow love is to APOLOGIZE AND RELEASE—release others for what you perceive they may have done to hurt you and apologize for what you may have done to hurt someone else (intentionally or unintentionally).

The last and most difficult step to grow love is to LOVE THE SELF, realizing we are all playing roles for each other. The perpetrator needed the victim, and the victim needed the perpetrator. You cannot truly love someone until you can love yourself first.

Remember...

No one can hurt you without your soul's permission. What you are experiencing today most likely was something you once did in the past. In God's eyes, there is no right, and there is no wrong. There is no good, and there is no bad. There are only experiences from which we grow.

The first step in healing is to accept what happened. As long as you are stuck in blame, shame, and guilt, you cannot heal. Acceptance is the first step in healing, followed by understanding what happened and why, and then change—your thoughts, beliefs, and behaviors.

You are a beautiful soul today because of all your past experiences. Honor and recognize the beauty within you. Look to find the beauty in others. We are all in this together.

An Example

I once worked with a man in his late 50s who was diagnosed with liver cancer. Liver holds extreme anger, and cancer is only an emotion (repressed anger) eating away at someone. His wife asked me to help him to heal so I asked her what had made this man (we'll call him Sam) so angry that it was eating away at him. She knew exactly what it was!

When Sam was a young boy, his father was an alcoholic and was physically and verbally abusive to him. When Sam turned nine, his mother divorced his father and remarried. Sam never saw his father again. He felt abandoned by his father.

Sam's stepfather was a kind and loving man who treated him well. Sam married a beautiful, loving young woman, and they had two beautiful, loving daughters. The more time passed, the angrier Sam would become with his father.

One of my gifts in healing is the ability to connect with one's soul to release emotions no longer needed. Sometimes we get stuck in our emotions. We wallow in self-pity. Imagine that emotion as a cookie in a cookie jar with a narrow opening. Unless we connect with that cookie, we will not be able to get it out. Similar situations in life are created to help us release. Unfortunately, instead of releasing, we only add to the cookies already collected.

Because Sam did not believe in past lives, his focus was on the current life. When I connected with Sam's soul, I learned Sam's anger was not really toward his father; it was toward himself. Sam unconsciously saw in his father the reflection of who he once was, and Sam didn't like it.

Unconsciously Sam was angry with himself because he once was the drunk who used to beat and verbally abuse his son, a man who later abandoned his son when he was just a child. Sam now knew what it felt like to be on the receiving end of abuse and abandonment, and it was painful! How could he have done this to someone, especially his own child? On a soul level, Sam couldn't forgive himself for what he had once done in another lifetime.

When I asked the soul why time did not heal this wound, the response received was: the more love Sam was shown, the more unworthy he felt of the love received.

Sam died not long after—his soul's choice. When he incarnates again, Sam will be the observer. He will know someone going through a similar situation so his heart can begin to heal through compassion.

There truly is no better way to learn than to receive back that which you once gave out. The Law of Karma helps us to become pure unconditional love on our evolutionary journey.

Lesson 4

Living Life

"Nearly all health problems, no matter what form they take or whatever name they have been given by the medical establishment, are caused by lack of harmony, imbalances and unresolved issues, past or present, in the emotional body. In order to heal the body, you must first heal the deep-seated feelings that cause the disturbances. When harmony in the emotional body is restored, the body will align easily and the healing you seek will become permanent." — Aurelia Louise Jones[40]

Spiritual Maladies

Every dis-ease is a spiritual malady. We have 18-24 hours to release a trauma or the trauma is stored in the spirit body to be resolved at a later date. Excess emotions held in the spirit body overflow into the physical body to reflect what is going on within, causing dis-ease.

Each body part holds a different emotion. For example, intestines store "old shit we no longer need," and kidneys hold feelings of being "pissed off." Grieving is held in the lungs, and extreme anger is held in the liver. Our legs move us forward in life; our feet are our foundation. The brain is our computer. Problems with the brain represent a wrong way of thinking.

Many serious, long-term dis-eases such as Parkinson's and muscular dystrophy can be karmic. For example, a client of mine had been a preacher in a past life and misused his power by mis-guiding his congregation. To balance this misuse of power, my client chose to experience a muscular dis-ease in his current life. Muscles represent power. Until the debt is balanced, the dis-ease will continue.

There are some dis-eases for which no cure will ever be found because they are spiritual in nature, such as SIDS, Alzheimer's, scoliosis. The universe does not punish or bless anyone. It merely responds to the vibration sent.

That which we view as a physical malady actually has its roots in the spiritual world. Look for the lesson in every experience to find the blessing.

Addiction

Addiction is a choice we make—either before coming into life or while in life. If we make the choice before coming in, we may have wanted to see if we could find the strength within to overcome the addiction so that we could have the compassion necessary to help others suffering from this same affliction. Someone who made the choice to experience addiction after birth has chosen to escape life—even if for a brief moment in time.

We all have our addictions, some more serious than others. For example, drama is an addition. An addict is someone who is dependent on a potentially harmful drug or behavior. The drug or behavior has control over that person.

Sensual pleasure can be intoxicating. Life is good, but reality eventually settles in. This temporary high only gives way to an equal low, an example of life's duality.

The only way to change a severely addictive behavior is through some type of 12-Step Recovery Program. Addicts need professional help. They cannot do it alone.

Don't be an enabler! An enabler is a person who, through their actions, allows an addict to continue his self-destructive behavior. Examples of enabling include: providing alcohol for the alcoholic, calling in "sick" when he misses work, giving him money (which will eventually go toward purchasing the substance), cleaning up his mess, and being in a state of denial (refusing to acknowledge the true state of the situation).

Enabling someone who makes poor life choices does not help them. An enabler is a "people pleaser." They "buy" love to win someone's attention or approval. Become the safety net so the lessons can be learned.

AIDS and Sexually-Transmitted Dis-eases

Acquired Immunodeficiency Syndrome (AIDS), sexually-transmitted dis-eases (STDs) and venereal dis-eases (VDs) result from beliefs of being unclean or unworthy imposed by others. Believing what other people think of you can show up as a dis-ease, created by the mind. If a child hears he is "bad" often enough, he will begin to believe it and cause trouble.

Before coming into life, we chose our sexual orientation. We also chose what we wanted to experience in life as well as what karma to balance.

When we are prejudiced against a particular group of people, we will be on the other end of the situation eventually (e.g., a future life). When we mistreat another human being or animal in any way, we will be on the other end of the situation. You cannot hurt another without hurting yourself.

Our negative thoughts do affect others. Thoughts are things. And when we vocalize our thoughts, they become more powerful; the effect is even more pronounced.

In a Group Channeling with Source/God through Elliott Eli Jackson several years ago, Source/God told the group: When you kill someone with a knife, you take their life. But when you kill someone with your words, they carry this hurt with them through the current lifetime and into the next, and the next, and the next, until it can be resolved. Source/God told us it is by far worse to kill someone's spirit than it is to kill someone with a knife. This made perfect sense to me.

God gave us free choice to be with whomever we want and to be whatever sexual orientation we want to be. But in order to create a child, it takes a man and a woman.

ADD and ADHD

Both Attention Deficit Disorder (ADD) and Attention Deficit and Hyperactivity Disorder (ADHD) affect the way a child thinks and behaves. The signs and symptoms are similar but vary. Children with ADD do not present signs of hyperactivity while children with ADHD do.

A child diagnosed with ADD or ADHD is a high energy being in a small body. An example would be to stuff an oversized sweater into a small box. There is nothing wrong with these children, but there is something wrong with the way we treat them.

These children are usually very smart and can have a high Intelligence Quotient (IQ). Teach these children how manage their energy through sports, puzzles, and other mind-challenging games. Make sure they eat healthy, organic food with little sugar and no preservatives. Preservatives and sugar are the leading causes of hyperactivity in children.

Prescription drugs hinder more than they help. You can raise your child without medication. It takes time and effort to keep these high-energy children off of medication, but if you truly love your child, you will do it. And yes, their body size will eventually catch up with their energy level.

Allergies

Some allergies are triggers to past traumas (current and past lives), and some may not have been properly diagnosed. Some people may think they have an allergy to something when, in fact, they do not. They believe they have an allergy based on symptoms listed on a television commercial or in a magazine ad. It may be based on what someone else said or had. A parent can diagnose a child with an allergy in the same way. No test is ever done to validate the allergy.

Seeds are planted daily by pharmaceutical companies wishing to sell pills. If someone believes strongly that they have a disease, the mind can create it. It can also be released.

Heal the past to heal the present. All of our memories, past and present, are stored in our energy field. The spirit body carries these memories from one lifetime to the next until the issue can be resolved. A past-life regression can be helpful to heal traumas from past lives. Examples include:

A client of mine who had been suffering from an allergy to grass learned she had been raped on a grassy knoll in a past life. She couldn't look at the man who was raping her so she looked at the grass. The grass was the trigger to the trauma she had not yet released.

Another client of mine had an allergy to mold. During a past-life regression we learned she had been wrongfully imprisoned in an old, dark, damp, musty cell and kept there for a long period of time. The trigger to the trauma was mold. My client released the trauma and her allergy to mold that day.

Alzheimer's Dis-ease

Alzheimer's is a spiritual gift. The soul of the afflicted individual takes on the dis-ease to help others learn compassion, patience, acceptance, and tolerance.

The dis-ease is a spiritual gift because it also provides an opportunity to balance karma. It can also provide an opportunity for family and loved ones to unite. Doctors and nurses balance karma and earn dharma (grace) by the attitude taken when helping an afflicted spirit. Always treat others in the same way you would want to be treated.

People with Alzheimer's revert back in time. They remember the good times, re-living those moments in their mind. Do this enough, and they will get stuck in the past. Over time they go back, further and further, until they become like babies who must be spoon fed. Eventually they are in the womb, forgetting how to swallow.

People who constantly live in the past have lost their purpose. The past is all they talk about. They feel stuck and slowly begin to withdraw from life. If you want to help a loved one who displays signs of Alzheimer's, try hard not to talk about the past or you will keep them there. Help them stay focused on the present and the future. Give them a reason and purpose to live. Once the dis-ease takes hold, it cannot be reversed.

Toward the end of the dis-ease, another spirit roaming the astral realm can take over the body. This explains why some Alzheimer's patients do things they would never have dreamt of doing. For example, someone who spent a life being prudish now runs around naked. The loved one's spirit is no longer there.

Anxiety and Depression

Impatience is a sign of anxiety. Anxiety is the need to control. Control is a sign of fear. Fear is a sign of not having surrendered to love. Love is everything. God is love. ~ Anonymous

There is no control in life—only choices and their resulting consequences. Our choices can be high vibrational or low vibrational. Either way, they are choices we make.

If we view anxiety and depression as a battle we cannot win, it will be. Energy is always in motion but it is not always flowing.

When energy is not flowing through us, it becomes stagnant and we become depressed. Energy must flow to maintain life.

Depression can be a spiritual malady. Someone experiencing depression has simply stepped off their spiritual path. They have forgotten their purpose in life. They are listening to the lower vibrations.

Antidepressants and anti-anxiety medication may work short-term, but they can cause a wide variety of health problems, including jitteriness, decreased sexual desire, nausea, weight gain, and insomnia. A study published in the journal *Frontiers of Psychology* reported depressed people who use antidepressants are far more likely to suffer a relapse of major depression than those who avoid antidepressants.[41]

Long-term, prescription drugs that treat depression and anxiety reduce brain functioning, deepen depression, and cause irrational behavior. Eventually, suicide may be a choice made by the afflicted individual.

The survival instinct within all of us is so strong that the psyche continues to deal with unnecessary stress, anxiety, and depression until that "self-preservation mechanism's strength is depleted and the urgency to escape further despair becomes overpowering. This happens to individuals who believe their personal or world circumstances are hopeless or are intensely grieving the loss of someone beloved."[42]

You don't need prescription drugs to help with depression, for they only mask the problem. They do not heal the root of the problem. Prescription drugs may help those around the individual, but they do not help the afflicted individual.

Research has proven that increased dopamine and serotonin levels in the body raise our level of joy.[43] Serotonin is the chemical of the brain that acts as a mood stabilizer, while dopamine is a neurotransmitter used by the nerves to send "messages." It allows us to have feelings of bliss, pleasure, euphoria, drive, motivation, focus, and concentration.

Our diet is a major contributing factor to the way we feel. Seven foods that could boost your serotonin are eggs, cheese, pineapples, tofu, salmon, nuts, and turkey.[44] (*See Tools for Healthy Living, Anxiety and Depression*)

Someone suffering from anxiety and depression must learn to find joy in life again. They must learn the difference between pleasure and happiness. Pleasure is for the moment. True happiness comes from within.

Anxiety and depression are signs of fallen angels affecting one's behavior. They drain your energy and whisper negative thoughts in your ear. The lower vibrations can twist our words, cause us to react with jealousy and anger, or convince us we are right and everyone else is wrong. Know when you are under the influence of low vibrations and work to release them!

Always look to find the beauty in life and the beauty within. You are important! Learn to be a little more selfish and less self-centered. To be selfish means to take time to care for you. If you don't, no one else will, and you will not be able to help someone who needs your help.

Asthma

The breath represents our ability to take in life. Someone with asthma, on some level, may be deciding whether or not life is worth living. Asthma can also be brought in from a past life, a trauma that needs to be healed.

Asthma may be a result of losing someone or something (through death or other means). We grieve when losing a loved one, job, marriage, or child who has left home. Some people grieve endlessly.

The person or thing that left may have been that person's identity. This often happens with caretakers who devote their life to caring for someone who is sick. Caretakers can lose sight of who they are if they do not take time for themselves. The asthma can become their new identity.

The person grieving may be holding on to feelings of blame, shame, guilt, or other unresolved issues with the person who left or has died. Asthma can be a form of self-punishment.

Autism and Similar Disorders

Children born with autism (not the result of vaccinations) and other unexplainable conditions, such as hypotonia (also known as "floppy baby syndrome") and Down syndrome chose to come into life this way. They chose their parents, and they chose their physical bodies.

These high-vibrational children came to help raise the vibration of the Earth by just being what they are—pure Light. They incur no karma. They are pure love, and they exude it. These children make us smile, and they open our hearts to love. Love and accept them for the beautiful souls they are.

Do not try to "fix" them, because you can't. Let them progress at their speed, not yours. They are happy where they are. We must allow the lessons to unfold and not try to force things the way we think they should be. There is a bigger picture always!

Make them comfortable and nurture them. Stimulate them, find ways to communicate with them, and have patience with them. Attend to their every need, for they are a blessing, even if at times it does not feel like it. Love them with all your heart!

These dear souls chose their parents for a reason. They knew they would be loved and accepted for who they are unconditionally. Parents and caretakers, have the patience and dedication it takes to help these children throughout their lifetime. They are a special gift, and that's why your child chose you. Not everyone could do what you do!

Inflammation and Infection

Infection in the body represents "infectious thoughts," and inflammation in the body represents "unshed tears." All pain is emotional. Discomfort in the body is a sign that something is wrong in the body.

True healing means taking time to see what is really going on within you to release all pain and dis-ease. Look at what happened right before the flare-up. There's your clue. Change your way of thinking, and you change your way of feeling.

Menstruation Problems

Women with menstruation problems, such as heavy bleeding, often have experienced a birthing trauma in a past life.

Years ago a friend of mine suffered from intense cramping (similar to labor pains), swollen breasts, and heavy bleeding during her menstrual cycle. Even though she was past menopause, the symptoms never ended.

Through a past-life regression we learned my friend was a slave (we'll call her Josie) in the southern United States. Her owner had impregnated Josie because his wife couldn't bear children and Josie's skin was light in color. No one would know the difference. The baby was to go to the slave owner's wife at birth so she would have a child of her own.

The owner and his wife arrived when it was time to deliver the baby. Josie could not bear the thought of losing her baby. Josie screamed repeatedly during pregnancy, "Please don't take my baby. Please don't take my baby." She died in childbirth, the result of hemorrhaging.

After the past-life regression, we did an energy healing session to release the stored trauma. Because we are spirits having a human experience, stored emotions must be released through the physical body.

When I placed my hands on my friend's pelvic area to send healing energy, my friend began to scream with labor pains, picking up where she once left off. The excessive bleeding and pain she experienced monthly since puberty was her unconscious mind trying to deliver the baby from this past life. In her mind, it was still with her.

So we pretended to deliver the baby. My friend pushed and I coached until the baby arrived. I cleaned the baby up, and then placed it on her chest. My friend said she could feel the baby's breath. Her soul was now at peace, and the symptoms never returned.

My friend was black in the past life and white in the present life. As part of our earthly experiences, we live in different races, cultures, and religions. There is something to be learned from all of them. Never be prejudiced against anyone. Sooner or later, you will be on the opposite end of what you once gave out (karma). Karma does not end with death. It carries over from one lifetime to another.

It matters not who you once were. What matters is who you are now and how you live your present life. Your past lives helped to create the person you are today. Heal the past to heal the present.

Mental Disorders

Bipolar disorder (manic-depression), multiple-personality disorder, and schizophrenia are viewed as mental illness, but in Truth, they are the result of one or more fallen angels taking over the physical body. Anxiety, depression, and addiction are signs of being under the influence of these lower vibrations.

People with bipolar disorder, a common mental disorder, can have alternating moods of mania and depression lasting for weeks or months at a time. Treatment involves medications that tend to make a person feel emotionless or like a zombie.

People with schizophrenia, a less common disorder, have both hallucinations (seeing or hearing things that are not there) and delusions (a belief in something that is not true). It is difficult for them to interact with others and to function well in society. They often wind up homeless. Treatment involves medication and psychotherapy.

People with multiple-personality disorder and schizophrenia are reported to hear voices that tell them what to do. They might experience sudden thoughts, impulses, or emotions the person has no control over.

It has been proven the personality change in multiple-personality disorder can trigger a change in the behavior, consciousness, memory, perception, cognition, and motor functions of the physical body. [45]

The negative thoughts and voices we hear in our head are the result of fallen angels. They know our weak spots, and they know how to play us. Work to release them.

A mental disorder can be compared to leaving a car with the motor running while the owner goes on vacation. Anyone can take the car for a drive wherever and however they want.

Menopause

Menopause takes place when the function of the ovaries ceases. Age is not a factor when menopause takes place. Symptoms include abnormal vaginal bleeding, hot flashes, vaginal and urinary symptoms, and mood changes. Women may notice they are not as easily aroused and may be less sensitive to the touch. This can lead to less interest in sex.

From a metaphysical perspective, the "change" in life takes place when a woman no longer accepts less than what she deserves in life. She is tired of taking care of everyone else, and now it is time to take care of her. She is important, and it's time for her and others know this. Her role in life has changed, and she is becoming a new person.

The best way to get through menopause is by having monthly energy healing sessions, such as Reiki. Energy healing can help to release that which you no longer need. It can re-balance and re-energize your bodies (physical, mental, emotional, and spiritual). It can help you to see things clearly.

This is how I and many others have gotten through menopause with ease and grace. We hardly knew menopause took place because we never experienced any of the "normal" symptoms of menopause.

The symptoms most people experience are signs that their energy is out of balance or their joy in life is leaving. It may be a sign that you are too sensitive or too overbearing. You may be holding on to feelings of being "pissed off" or anger toward your mate. Pay attention to what your body is telling you.

A monthly energy healing session is recommended for everyone to keep our energy in balance and to send away the low vibrations that whisper in our ear. Treat yourself to one today. You'll be amazed at what it can do for you!

Post-Traumatic Stress Disorder (PTSD)

PTSD is the name given to a condition that can develop after experiencing or witnessing one or more life-threatening events, like combat, a natural disaster, a car accident, or sexual assault. It is deeply rooted within the spirit body.

Safety is the first step in healing PTSD. Until one can feel safe, healing cannot take place. And until you know what happened in a past life, you cannot heal it. Any little thing in the present life can trigger a trauma from the present or past life. Like a weed, if you do not get to the root, it will come back thicker and stronger. PTSD cannot be completely healed until all of the unseen traumas are healed.

Quantum Healing Hypnosis Therapy (QHHT) works extremely well to help heal PTSD. Here the Higher Self can be accessed. The Higher Self knows the answers to everything. It knows the plan we came in with in this life. It knows our contracts with other people. It knows everything about us. It has access to the records of the collective consciousness, past and present. Insight into past lives for us and others can be found here. Healing can also take place while in this state.

Not everyone can go into a deep trance, known as the somnambulistic state. Many people with PTSD cannot be hypnotized because they do not want to see the trauma causing their condition. For people with PTSD, it is best a surrogate be used to gain the appropriate information and the best way to heal them.

The Emotional Freedom Technique (EFT), Tapas Acupressure Technique (TAT), and The Emotion Code can also be helpful to release PTSD.

Scoliosis

Scoliosis occurs after the age of nine when we receive our karmic package. The karmic package arrives in the form of a ball of energy.

When "opened," this ball of energy disseminates into the body's energy field to be balanced at a later date. The spirit receiving the karmic package may think, "Life is good. Why open it now and ruin everything?" If the spirit refuses to "open" the package, the spirit pushes it "to the back" where it will stay until the spirit accepts responsibility for what it once created.

The spine was made to be flexible, and this flexibility includes the ability to wrap around a ball of energy (even if we do not see it). When the karmic package is pushed to the back, the vertebrae wrap around the ball of energy, resulting in curvature of the spine.

The sooner the karmic package is opened, the sooner the spine will straighten. If we wait too long, the bones become hardened or "set" because we have become inflexible or "set" in our way of thinking.

Suicide

Suicide is a choice we make—either before coming into life or while in life. Suicide can be karmic. Someone who commits suicide in one life will have to balance the experience by knowing someone who committed suicide in another life.

One of my clients had watched his father, brother, and son commit suicide at different times in the exact same way in the same lifetime. His sea of emotion was overwhelming. Through a past-life regression, we learned he was the one who had committed suicide in front of his father, brother, and son. We healed the present by healing the past.

Threatening suicide is a way to gain attention and creates karma. Work to heal you. If you try to commit suicide and it is not your time to go Home, it will not happen. Someone will interrupt your plan, or you will end up with a damaged physical body.

Spiritual Truths

The foundation of man, the core of who we really are, is being ripped apart to help us remember who we really are, individually and collectively. Lies, greed, prejudices, jealousy, envy, and all of our fears are being exposed to be rectified and healed through that which we are—Love.

The true Armageddon (the internal storm of accepting that which is Truth and that which is not) is being reflected in the earth; e.g., sink holes, large cracks and craters, earthquakes, and volcanic eruptions. The Light always exposes and overcomes darkness. The vibration of the earth is rising. Mother Earth is bringing in a new world. She is in labor, and these physical pains can be likened to birthing pains.

Wisdom that never changes is a Spiritual Truth. While there are many spiritual truths, here are a few I feel are important to the understanding of life:

Love and Fear

There are only two root emotions in life—love and fear. Fear is the absence of love. Where fear exists, love cannot. It is impossible to love that which you fear. If we fear God, we cannot love God. When we feel love, we feel connected to God. When fear is present, we feel disconnected. God is pure love; fear is man-made.

Every emotion we experience stems from either love or fear. Positive emotions create happiness, joy, peace, gratitude, and serenity. Negative emotions create anger, jealousy, envy, self-centeredness, judgment, and disdain, to name a few. When experiencing a negative emotion, we must ask ourselves why we are afraid. Fears must be faced. The only way to conquer a fear is by moving through it, not running away from it.

Recognize your fears; don't deny them. What are you getting out of the situation in which you experience this fear? If you weren't getting something out of it, you wouldn't be in it. What are your boundaries? What will you allow, and what won't you allow? Without boundaries, there is no self-respect or self-worth.

Fear can be the result of a trauma in the past (current or past life). For example, someone who is afraid of drowning may have drowned in a previous lifetime. Fear can be rooted in the idea of losing someone or something. Someone who is worried about whether or not a spouse will cheat on him or her has probably cheated on someone in the past.

Fear can be a learned behavior. It can be instilled in us as a result of a parent's behavior. For example, a parent who is afraid of animals or afraid to take a chance in life can instill this behavior in their child.

And then, there is the fear of feeling alone, unwanted, and unloved. Heal the trauma so you can move through the fear.

Where fear begins, love ends. Before we can love another, we must first love ourselves. What is your relationship with yourself? Everything begins and ends with you.

Energy Follows Attention

The more attention we give something, the more we create it. The more we believe something to be true, the faster we bring it into being. If we think we are going to catch a dis-ease (e.g., the flu), we will create it. The only thing "catchy" is a thought.

If we think about living a life centered on love, if we believe in such a life, then we can create it for ourselves. When we live a life rooted in love, we live a long and healthy life. If our life is rooted in fear, our bodies break down and dis-ease will settle in to show us what is going on within.

When you place your faith and trust outside of yourself, thinking someone else knows more than you or is better than you, you give that person your power. They grow stronger, and you grow weaker; their ego is fed while your self-worth slips away.

A simple thought can uplift someone, or it can tear them down. Thoughts are things, and every thought will come back to its source in the positive or negative manner in which it was given out, tenfold. Energy gains momentum as it works its way back to you.

Your world was created by your thoughts. Our words and actions validate our thoughts; they are more powerful. If you don't like your world, change your way of thinking.

Past Lives

Past lives do exist, and they do have an effect on us.

Birth marks are a sign of stored trauma, usually from past lives. We chose to bring them in as a badge of honor or a reminder of a trauma from a past life that needs healing. They can even be a reminder of what not to do on an unconscious level. For example, my small frame and tiny wrists (smaller than a child's) are the result of a past life when I was starved, raped, tortured, and experimented on for being Jewish. And there is a birth mark on my left arm where an arrow almost killed me in another life.

Vows and heartfelt promises made in previous lifetimes are

carried into future lives if not consciously released. For example, someone who was a priest or nun and took a vow of celibacy in a past life will have trouble experiencing a successful relationship in a future life. Everything is energy. The energy of the vow is still vibrating in their energy field.

Someone who took a vow of poverty in a past life will have trouble attaining prosperity in another life. Someone who promised to wait for a loved one "forever and ever" until they can be together again in a past life will have trouble having a successful relationship in another life because unconsciously, he or she is still waiting for that same special someone to come. Take time to release all vows and promises so you can live life to its fullest.

To release past vows and promises, write a letter to yourself releasing all vows, promises, and lovers from the past—anything that is negatively affecting your current life. Read it out loud (validation), burn it (purification), then toss the ashes to the earth (release). Everything in life is symbolic.

At any given time, you are the sum total of all your past lives. The world you know today is a result of what you created in the past and what you are creating in the present. If you don't like your world, change it by changing you. And when you change, your world will change with you.

Life is all about choices. Situations will be presented for you to learn your lessons. When we come to a fork in the road, there will always be a choice to make. If the choice is made in fear, you will have another opportunity to repeat the lesson to make the choice in love.

Whatever you think, say, or do, do it with love. Always do what is for the best and highest good for all concerned, not just for the self. This is so important and cannot be stressed enough. So many people in the world today think not of anyone but themselves. This must change if the world is to change. It's time to become "other" centered instead of "self" centered.

There is more to you than you will ever know. Like a diamond, you are a multi-faceted, multi-dimensional being. Never be afraid to learn more about you. We learn from our mistakes. God does not judge and neither should we. Love yourself for the person you have become, not for who you once were!

Abandonment and Betrayal

When you peel off the many layers of hurt and the traumas from the past, you will find a lack of trust in God. We no longer trust that God will supply us with everything we need; we no longer trust the process of life.

Abandonment and betrayal are at the root of all our fears, and both have to do with our relationship with God. We feel God has abandoned and betrayed us (on an unconscious level) when we needed Him/Her most, but it is really we who abandoned and betrayed God. God has never abandoned or betrayed us. We are always connected to God, even if we don't feel it at times. When we don't feel God's presence in our lives, it is because we are blocking God.

Change your relationship with God, and you will change your relationship with yourself and others.

Greed and Competition

When fear is present, look at the lack or loss causing the fear. Those who are jealous are afraid of losing something or someone. Those who are envious want for what they wish they could have or be. Competition is an issue, even if it is one-sided.

Those who feel as if they have no control in their lives try to control and manipulate others. Those who are greedy are afraid they will never have enough. They use manipulation as a tool to control others to get what they want. Greed is rampant in mankind in every aspect of life when it comes to money, power, fame, or love. It is an intoxicating drug that can become addictive.

A very wealthy friend of mine once told me it's not the money rich people aspire to acquire; it's the power that comes with it. Most people view wealthy people as powerful and like to ride on their coattails. Because of this inaccurate way of thinking, people can be bought, individually and collectively within a government. "Everyone has their price," we hear them say.

Judgment ensues when we compare ourselves and others. There is always a winner and a loser in a competition. People are not viewed as equal. Competition and greed can create peer and internal pressures, which can be unbearable at times.

Competition and greed, no matter how you choose to look at them, are not healthy. They are the downfall of any great nation or individual.

Karma

Mankind has individual, as well as collective, karma to balance. For example, a country that wars upon will be the country warred upon. A country that basks in gluttony will experience famine. What we give out, we will get back.

If you do not handle a situation from a place of love, you will get another opportunity to try again. A lesson will keep coming to you until you have learned it. A lesson may be repeated, taking it to a deeper level. Pay attention when you find yourself saying, "Why does this keep happening to me?" Instead ask, "What is it I need to learn from this?" Learn the lesson so you can move onto the next.

Liken your lessons to that of a child learning to tie his shoelaces. The child cries out "I can't do it!" while learning the lesson, but once the skill is mastered, the child rarely ever complains—the lesson is done automatically, without thinking. That which was once challenging is now done with ease.

How we handle an experience will affect what happens to us when the experience is balanced, and we are on the other side of the experience. For example, if you were rich and used your money for your own self-gain, you will not get much help in a lifetime when you are poor. If you were rich and used your money to help mankind with no thought of remuneration (dharma, also known as grace), you will receive help in a lifetime when you are poor. The amount of help given out will reflect the amount of help received when poor. No good deed ever goes unnoticed.

If we seek to be recognized for something we did in life, we will not receive recognition for it when we go Home. There is no "double dipping" when it comes to balance. The reward we receive when we go Home will be far greater than anything we could have received on Earth.

There are no guarantees in life. Live life the best you can while you are here. You are not responsible for what others do to you, but you are responsible for how you handle what happens to you.

Lower Vibrations

Just because you can't see something does not mean it doesn't exist. You can't always see electricity, but you can feel it when you stick your finger in an electrical outlet.

Everything in the universe is made up of energy vibrating at different frequencies. Something that looks solid is made up of vibrational energy fields at a quantum level.

Lower vibrations are real, and they can be felt. The pain in your neck or the pain that moves around on your body can be the result of a lower vibration. If it is a lower vibration, the pain will go away immediately. *(See Tools for Protection)*

Lower vibrations can attach themselves to us, affecting our behavior. The lower vibrations whisper thoughts that keep us from doing that which we should be doing. They keep us from moving forward on our spiritual path. They keep us in a state of depression, anxiety, addiction, and other mental maladies. They keep us from eating healthy and exercising. They keep us from prayer and meditation. They keep us stuck in the ego, greed, and self-centeredness.

Lower vibrations can also possess a body when someone wants to escape life. It's a game they play, and if allowed, you become their pawn. Sometimes lower vibrations must be removed through exorcism. Do not try to do this on your own.

Lower vibrations are everywhere. They can be likened to pollution in the air we breathe. You can't see them, but you can feel them. Do the best you can to protect yourself from them. Recite out loud the mantra to release lower vibrations, followed by The Platinum Shield for protection. Raise your vibration by reciting out loud the Great I Am Discourses given to us from Source/God through Elliott Eli Jackson.

Work to maintain a high vibration to keep the lower vibrations away.

The Key to Life is Balance

When we are in balance, everything flows and synchronicity takes place. When we are out of balance, we feel our world is out of control. We often try to control others. Our inner world must be in balance with our outer world.

When there is chaos in our life, there is chaos within. When there is peace within, there is peace in our life. Find your peace; peace is love.

When one of your bodies is out of alignment, they are all out of alignment (domino effect). When we feel blocked or "stuck," our energy is not flowing properly. Nothing flows in our lives.

Like a battery, we are made up of polar opposites to help us learn our lessons. We are positive and negative, masculine and feminine. All of our bodies must be in balance for life to flow smoothly.

Masculine energies are the thinking, intellectual, doing, thrusting, seeking elements of our natures, and they are necessary for us to grow and accomplish. Feminine energies are the healing, intuitive, creative, wise, accepting, being elements. When the masculine and feminine energies within an individual are balanced, that person is whole.

The key to life is balance. Many of us have issues around

money. Having too little money or too much money can both cause problems in our life. They are two sides of the same coin; both create fear in our life—fear of losing or not having enough money. The issue is the same; the perspective is different. Money is not the problem; the amount of it is.

For example, water is water. Too much water and you have a flood. Too little water and you have a drought. Water is not the problem; the amount of water is.

In life, we may need to learn the balance between being greedy and indifferent or between hoarding and squandering. We may need to learn the balance between seriousness and fun, work and play, giving and receiving in all areas of life. Balance is a major life lesson.

Power without wisdom is dangerous. Wisdom is applied knowledge. When wisdom and power are in balance, we live in harmony with ourselves and other people.

Visualize a glass of water. The glass represents the relationship between two people. The water and the air represent the two people in the relationship. As you drink of the water, the ratio of water to air changes. As one person changes, the other person has to change along with them. When you change, your world will change with you.

And when the water and air are in equal amounts in the glass, they are in balance. When the two people agree on a similar way of thinking or being, the relationship is in balance.

The Law of the Circle

The Law of the Circle is also known as the Law of Cause and Effect or the Law of Karma. This law teaches that for every cause there is an unstoppable effect. A good example of cause and effect would be that of a child who places his hand on a hot stove and gets burnt. Touching the stove is the "cause," and the resulting burn is the "effect." In doing so, the child learns to avoid burning himself in the future by not touching the stove and thereby circumventing the effect. It is through our mistakes that we learn what not to do.

In the book *Teachings for the New Golden Age*, Ascended Master Kuthumi teaches the Law of the Circle by stating that energy, magnetized and used, must return to the sender. If the energy was used constructively, it will return as happiness. If the energy was used destructively, it will return to the sender as misery in the same way it was given out.[46]

The Law of the Circle teaches that every new endeavor must begin from within, the core essence of the Creator, and return to within. In other words, what you sow is what you reap. Whatever you give out, you will get back in the very same way it was given out. This law applies to just about every experience in life. If you are on the receiving end now, most likely you have been on the giving end previously. Don't shoot the messenger!

In Truth, there is no right or wrong, good or bad. There are only high-vibrational choices and low-vibrational choices.

Energy cycles and gains momentum along its path; energy will return tenfold as a result. The more positive you are, the more "good" things happen. The more negative you are, the more "bad" things happen. By changing a thought pattern, you can undo that which you would have to experience. Be careful with what you give out. You may not like what you get back!

Every life experience is exactly what you need in order to find out more about you or a God virtue (e.g., strength, perseverance, courage) you have chosen to learn. Everyone and everything in life is a mirror back to you, for it is through another that you see what is taking place within you.

Your physical body is a reflection of you as well. Negative thoughts come back in the way of life lessons or dis-ease. There are no accidents in life. There is always a reason and a purpose for everything that happens.

Abundance and Prosperity

Abundance and prosperity are our birthright. Mankind has been struggling with a poverty consciousness created by our own beliefs in lack and limitation for a very long time. This false belief system has held us in the grip of fear, poverty, greed, self-centeredness, and corruption.

Money has been a source of pain and suffering throughout history. Religion has considered money to be the "root of all evil," yet the Bible teaches "The love of money is the root of all evil. Some men in their passion for it have strayed from the faith, and have come to grief amid great pain." (1 Timothy 6:10)[47]

Poverty keeps us from fulfilling our Divine plans. To live a life of poverty is demeaning and humiliating. It is painful and causes suffering. Poverty is the root of many of our problems: physical, mental, and emotional. We can do more good and help more people if we have money than if we don't have money.

Man's self-centered desire for greed and power has been around for thousands of years, corrupting societies and governments.

In our many past lives, we may have either abused our wealth or others may have used their wealth to abuse us. We may have taken vows of poverty. These etheric records still vibrate at a sub-conscious level and can keep us from attracting prosperity. It is a pattern that needs to be broken; but like any pattern, it takes time and practice to change a habit.

Women are the True Leaders

"A woman's highest calling is to lead a man to his soul,
so as to unite him with Source. Her lowest calling is
to seduce, separating man from his soul and leave
him aimlessly wandering. A man's highest calling
is to protect woman, so she is free to walk the earth
unharmed. Man's lowest calling is to ambush and force
his way into the life of a woman." ~ Cherokee Proverb[48]

In Truth, women are the leaders and men are the protectors. Women have forgotten their role because men have tried to control and manipulate women through the ages through religion, politics, and peer pressure.

Women make great leaders because they are compassionate and nurturing. They are good at multi-tasking and are great listeners. They are flexible and can defy all odds. Women make strong, effective leaders because they focus on teamwork and are motivated by challenges. They will find a solution to settle an argument without fighting over the principle. They think twice before sending children off to war.

Men work to protect their families from those who wish to harm them. They protect their family by providing food, clothing, and education. They protect their family's self-esteem and self-worth, their way of life, and they guard against any threats to things that their family values. The hardest part of being a protector is to know when to protect someone and when to allow someone to learn their lesson. Self-esteem and independence come from achievements, large and small. To meet life's challenges and come out on top builds the confidence to stand alone and have a life, and to share a life.

The masculine energy has ruled the planet for thousands of years, and now the feminine energy is returning. Women are reclaiming their power.

Both masculine and feminine energies must be balanced within each of us, individually and collectively. Look around and you see more men staying home to take care of their children while their spouses work. Some men's breasts are becoming more pronounced (men even get breast cancer), and some women are getting hair in their facial and chest areas.

When women begin to remember their true roles, life will change for the better. Women, remember your husbands and children want to feel loved. Love is felt through the kiss, a hug, heartfelt sentiments, and hands that are held. The tissues in your hands are the same as those in your heart. Love is spread through the touch. Women, lead your family well so they never stray. The joy and love you once gave out will be returned to you tenfold.

Men, empower your women. Uplift and support them as you would want to be uplifted and supported. Never belittle and degrade them. Women are your equal.

Choose your battles. You do not always have to be right. If

you are right, don't rub it in. Do not manipulate and control your other. Talk to your other; they cannot read your mind. Guide them, and then allow the outcome to take place knowing you've done the best you can. If the outcome is not what you expected, remember everything happens for a reason and a purpose.

Expectations and attachments (to people and things) are the root of all suffering. Plant seeds for what you would like to take place, and allow those seeds to take root. You may be surprised at the outcome!

Bringing about Change

We all want life to be different than it is, but too often we don't want to do the work to make life different. We want change to happen on its own. Like true healing, change begins within and moves outward. Change begins with each individual. We cannot change anyone else, but we can change ourselves.

Change takes place gradually, with intention and courage. Change brings about spiritual growth; it brings about maturity. The more you let go of past hurts, the softer you will become.

Unless you have a burning desire within to bring about change, it simply will not happen. You are the only one who can make it happen. No one else can or will do it for you—not even God.

Mistaking Pleasure for Happiness

Happiness is a state of well-being and contentment that comes from within, while **pleasure** is the joy we experience in reaction to special events (such as winning the lottery, getting a raise, or celebrating a birthday).

Most humans look for happiness outside themselves through pleasurable situations, but no matter how much pleasure we experience, it will never be enough if we are not happy with who we are.

External conditions and events provide pleasure, but true happiness comes from within. In order to find lasting happiness, we must have a good self-esteem and a life purpose. We need to know who we are and where we are going in life.

Stand strong in your beliefs, even when no one else does. Most people don't like to go against the status quo. A true leader can because their belief is strong.

From time to time, you may have to adjust your beliefs to make sure they are based in Absolute Truth, not just your perception of what truth is. Are you working for the very best and highest good for all concerned, or you working strictly for the self?

Is what you want a "must have" or a "want"? The danger comes from when we want for more than what we need.

Learn to master your emotions. Respond, don't react. If you don't learn to detach from your emotions, you will drown in them. No one can make you feel bad except yourself. If you feel it in your gut (you get upset), your reaction is a result of your own fears. Look into the mirror.

Life is all about choices. Choose to live a happy life instead of a miserable life. The choice is always yours.

Adopt the Attitude of Gratitude. The more you give gratitude for something, the more you will receive of the same. There is nothing that will shift you faster than spending three to five minutes in gratitude. To appreciate more what you have in life, give gratitude. There's nothing better for the soul than an attitude of gratitude.

Live in the moment. Release the past, look towards the future, live in the present. All you have is now. You can't go back in time to change anything. You can't experience something that hasn't happened. Learn to live in the now.

Honesty is always the best policy! Even when we tell a white lie, a part of us knows we are not being truthful. Dishonesty can damage your self-esteem because you are being dishonest with yourself. We hurt others when we lie, and we hurt ourselves as well. You cannot hurt someone else without hurting you. We are all connected.

Stay positive. Life was never meant to be easy. Earth is a school where we learn lessons. We don't grow through the good times; we grow through adversity. We create our life through our thoughts, words, and deeds. If you don't like your life, change it. No one else can or will do it for you.

Many people strive to be rich because they believe money can buy happiness. This is not true. You are rich when you are content and happy with who you are and what you have.

Happiness is being in service. There is no greater reward than the feeling of knowing you were able to help someone. Happiness comes from being "other"-centered instead of "self"-centered.

Pleasure can be found outside of the self, but it does not last. True happiness comes from within, and it is everlasting.

Boundaries

There are four important words in life: love, honesty, truth, and respect. Without these in your life, you have nothing. Boundaries are a sign of respect. They are a sign that you respect yourself, and when you respect yourself, others will respect you, too.

Healthy personal boundaries are required for a lasting relationship. Boundaries are for your protection; they should have consequences (cause and effect). The only people who get upset about you setting boundaries are those who were benefiting from you having none.

Boundaries set should have consequences. Consequences should be fair and enforced. There is no reason to set a boundary if it will not be enforced. Without consequences, your words become meaningless.

Without healthy boundaries, we allow people to take advantage of us. Co-dependent relationships have no boundaries because both partners believe they cannot live without the other.

A co-dependent relationship is a pattern of behavior where one partner makes sacrifices, real or imagined, for the other partner's happiness, looking for approval. They give endless support to their partner, even at the cost of their own mental, emotional, and physical health.

The receiving (weaker) partner depends on the giving (stronger) partner for just about everything from caregiving to bill paying to making meals and running errands. Physical, mental, and emotional control are exerted over the receiving partner because the receiving partner is afraid the giving partner will leave. The giving partner is often criticizing, overbearing, and demanding one minute and loving the next.

At the time, the receiving partner feels a sense of purpose and may appear to be self-sacrificing when in reality they may be avoiding their own unhappiness and personal issues. Eventually they lose their self-worth, thereby lowering their self-esteem. The receiving partner believes they are not getting much in return, but they really are getting something (such as financial security or shared religious or political beliefs) out of the situation or they wouldn't stay in the relationship.

In a co-dependent relationship, both parties are getting something from the other for fulfillment, even if it doesn't appear that way on the surface. Look deeper. As long as both parties are getting something out of the relationship, they will be together. If the relationship is karmic, both parties will stay together until the debt is done. If the relationship is healthy and loving when the debt is balanced, stay in it. If there is no love when the debt is over, leave. More karma is created by staying in the relationship than by leaving. This karma will have to be balanced yet again.

People who lack boundaries have low self-esteem. They cannot communicate directly and honestly. They become dependent on others, being controlled and manipulated by how others think, feel, and act toward them. They are fearful of rejection and conflict. They often have an inner child that needs healing. A person without boundaries cannot love him or herself.

Healthy relationships are not possible without proper communication. Tell people how you feel, and listen to them when they talk about their feelings. Compromise can bring an out-of-balance relationship back into balance.

When setting boundaries, keep in mind what is the highest and best good for all concerned—not just you.

Confronting Fear

Where fear exists, love cannot. Fear is the absence of love. If you cannot recognize your fears, how will you ever overcome them? If you cannot recognize your weaknesses, how will you ever make them your strengths?

Fear is something we create, and it can be paralyzing and painful. Fear is what stops us from moving forward in life; it keeps us from creating change. Fear itself is more terrifying than the experience we fear. When we resist change as a result of fear, life can become painful. There is nothing in life worth the pain we allow ourselves to experience.

We have more fear in our lives than we realize. When we say, "I'm afraid....," this is fear. Worrying is fear. Worrying is like praying for something you don't want.

What you resist persists. The more you resist, the more painful the experience. Where there is pain, there is fear.

Love is powerful; fear is destructive. Without love, life is not worth living. Fear is the only thing that stops us in life. So why do we continue to exist in a state of fear?

Worry is fear. Worrying about someone does not help that person. You only make things worse for them by projecting your fear toward them. Fear is negative energy, and your negative energy can bring that person down. The only thing that heals is love; send love.

Fear is the result of a trauma. For example, someone who has drowned in a past life may have a fear of drowning in the current life.

The energy of fear can be used constructively to move through a challenging situation. For example, if you are drowning, it can save your life. Fear can give you the extra energy required to make it to shore, such as "I will not drown." Find strength through your fear.

If you did not write a specific trauma into your life plan, it will not happen unless you create it—the result of fear or not listening to your inner guidance. Energy is magnetized. We attract to us exactly what we need.

When you fear something will happen to a loved one (a situation or dis-ease), you make life worse for your loved one because you send your negative thoughts into their energy field. Send love instead. Surround your loved one in the emerald green light of healing or the magenta light of unconditional love. Love is the only thing that heals. Love one another.

Pessimists live in fear. They find it difficult to be positive. Be the optimist who always looks on the bright side of what is happening.

Fear is the most destructive energy in the universe.

Letting Go of Anger

Anger is a byproduct of shame, blame, guilt, rejection, betrayal, and abandonment. If not released, it can turn into hatred.

Let's face it! We all get angry from time to time. We don't like what we see taking place in society, and it angers us. Justified anger expressed in a peaceful way brings about change.

Sometimes we get angry over situations for which we had no control. When we feel like we have no control in life, we try to control others. Control is a misnomer. There is no control in life; only choices. If you are going to the mall and an accident ahead of you brings you to a standstill, did you have control over the situation? No, but you do have a choice to stay where you are until the accident clears or to take a different route. The destination is the same no matter which route you take.

We get angry when physical situations take place in our life we feel we had no control over, such as a debilitating dis-ease or condition or a crime that took place. Both are karmic. What we forget is there are no victims in life—only co-creators of circumstances. You are on the receiving end of a situation because of what you once gave out (present or past life). The anger you feel is toward yourself on an unconscious level because now you know what it feels like to be on the other end.

If not released, repressed anger can become cancer in the physical body to reflect what is taking place within. Cancer eats away at the body just as anger eats away at us. If you look at cancer cells under a microscope, they look angry. To release cancer, release the anger stored within. If you cannot do this, the cancer in your body will return to show you what is going on within.

Instead of focusing on anger, focus on what made you angry and work to heal it. We can't change the past, but we can change the way we deal with it. Look for the gift in the experience; there are always gifts. What have you learned from it? What can you change within you so there is no need to repeat the lesson?

Work to resolve all issues before you or someone else dies. If you don't, the guilt and regret will haunt you until you do. Another lifetime will be created for you to do so. We are tied to each other eternally until we resolve the issue.

Apologize to yourself for what you once did. Apologize to others for what you may have done to them. It's never too late to do this. If that person has gone Home, write an apology letter. Their soul and yours will be grateful. *(See Appendix)*

Acceptance is the first step in healing. Accept what happened and work to heal it. If you're stuck in blame, shame, and guilt, you cannot heal. Take time to really look at the self; reflect upon what happened and why you drew the situation to you. You can't change what happened, but you can change the way you feel about it.

Building Self-Worth

Self-worth comes from within. When you stop comparing yourself to others, you will begin to see the value in you. You are judging yourself for what you are not. No two souls are alike. We are all unique and special. Do your best and then let it be. The greatest way to doubt you is to compare yourself to others.

Never see yourself as greater or less than another. How others view you and speak about you is important, but not as much as how you feel about yourself. Stop putting yourself down! You are a beautiful soul with many gifts to share. Share these gifts with people who need them. You begin to make a difference in the world when you begin to love yourself.

Stop creating yourself around what other people think you should be. This only creates inner conflict; you will never know who you really are or what you can achieve.

You will continue to suffer if you have an emotional reaction to everything that is said to you. True power is sitting back and observing everything from a different perspective. True power is restraint. If words control you, everyone else can control you as well. Breathe and allow things to pass.

What are your weaknesses? If you do not know your weaknesses, how will you ever make them your strengths? What are your fears? If you do not know your fears, how will you ever overcome them? What do you want to do in life? If you do not know where you are going, you will never be able to get there.

What areas of your life would you like to improve? What emotions would you like to release? What mistakes do you tend to repeat? Where do you tend to get stuck? Where do you regularly let yourself down? We all have our weaknesses and fears, we all face our own personal struggles, and we all need to work through them.

What are your strengths? These are your gifts. What are your abilities? What are you really good at? What do you want to be good at? Your strengths will help to build self-confidence and allow you to move forward with greater self-assurance. When you use your gifts to help others, you stop focusing on your own inadequacies.

Do not rely on other people to tell you what you are good at. If you truly believe with all your heart, that's all that matters. You will always find someone who doesn't like you or doesn't agree with you. It's a part of life—to help us know what we want and what we don't want in life, who we want to be and who we don't want to be.

"To thine own self be true," said Polonius in William Shakespeare's play *Hamlet*. Apologize to yourself for not accepting you for who you really are. You have never done anything wrong. You may have made mistakes along the way, but haven't we all?

Learn to love and accept yourself fully for the beautiful soul you are and for what you have become on your journey. At any time you are the sum total of all your past life experiences. The soul is already perfect, but your spirit is working on perfection.

True value does not come from the amount of money you have, your job status, what size house you have and its location, your social or relationship status. Self-worth comes from within, and it begins with self-confidence. Confidence is gained through much practice.

Love is the most powerful energy in the universe. Find something you love to do and do more of it. Then find something else you love to do and do more of it. The more you begin to focus on what you love to do, the more you will begin to value yourself. Build your house on a solid foundation, one brick at a time.

Lesson 5

You Create Your World

Most people do not want to look at themselves because we don't want to admit we aren't perfect. We cannot fathom that we would or could do anything to hurt someone else, and yet we have. It's easier to shoot the messenger and remain the victim than it is to admit we were wrong or made a mistake.

We created our world and everything in it through our thoughts, words, beliefs, and actions—in this life and in past lives. You will never understand the world around you if you cannot understand the world within. So if you don't like what you see, change you. And when you change, your world will change with you.

"The thought manifests as the word.
The word manifests as the deed.
The deed develops into habit.
And the habit hardens into character.
So watch the thought and its ways
with care. And let it spring from love
born out of concern for all beings.
As the shadow follows the body,
As we think, so we become."
~ Buddha[49]

You Create Your World

Thoughts are things. We have millions of thoughts running through our minds continually. You cannot shut down the mind; it is a part of you. But we can slow down the mind by refocusing our negative thoughts and our attention.

A thought flows in and out unless a belief is attached to it. Our world is created through our beliefs. We validate our thoughts through our words and actions. The more we believe in a thought, the more emotion we put into it. The amount of emotion you put into a belief will determine the outcome.

Energy follows attention. The more we focus on something we believe, the more energy we give it, the faster we create it. The more powerful and vivid the thoughts, the clearer the picture we give our mind and what we want it to do. This is why we should never worry.

There are only two root emotions in life: love and fear. The force of love can heal the planet. Where fear exists, love cannot. It is impossible to love that which you fear.

Remember that worrying draws to us that which we do not want. Focus on what you want in life instead of what you don't want. Keep your thoughts positive. Send love for a positive outcome.

Our moods and thoughts reflect the level of our energy. Our energy is high when we feel happy, positive, and loving. When our energy is low, we feel depressed, sad, and lonely. There is one sure way to change the way we feel—raise our level of energy. Do something you love to do, go for a walk, get together with friends, or play uplifting music. You're never stuck unless you're getting something out of the way you are feeling. Learn to control your energy and the underlying behavior patterns to bring about a change in you.

Our thoughts and emotions emit the same color, feeling, energy, or thought in others. Like a magnet, we attract that same energy back into our lives. Everything we send out into the universe comes back in the same way, thus explaining the saying "like attracts like."

When we totally accept someone for who they are, we allow them the space to grow safely. There are no accidents or coincidences in life. Everything happens for a reason and a purpose. We draw to us people, events, and situations to show us what is going on within us. We attract that which we fear most so that we may learn what they are and to overcome them.

Those who are kind and gentle may attract something violent to them because of a deep anger or unresolved issue (karma) within them. The issue may be something from the current or a past life. Accept it for what it is and move on. If you seek revenge, it will only come back to you for the lesson to be repeated again.

Life is what you make of it. You created your world through your thoughts, words, and actions. If you don't like what is taking place in your world, change it by changing you.

Self-Awareness

Take time to know your likes, dislikes, strengths, and fears. Stop trying to recreate yourself according to what someone else wants you to be. You'll never know all you can be until you take time to look into the mirror.

Where are you giving your power away? When you put

someone up on a pedestal, you give them your power. Never give your power away; it weakens the core.

What are your fears? Be honest. We all have more fears than we could imagine. Life's lessons have to do with letting go of fear and reconnecting with love.

What traumas have taken place in your life? Maybe what happened was to teach you strength or to stand up for yourself. Look for the gift in the situation. Some of the most challenging times in our life help clear the path so the most wonderful things can happen.

Of whom are you jealous or envious? What can you do to change you so you won't feel this way?

Know that no one can arouse anger, hurt, frustration, or irritation within you unless there is an unresolved issue within you. Violence is a manifestation of anger. Accidents, fires, and explosions are drawn to us as a result of our anger. When the entire household is burning mad, it can manifest as a house fire.

There are no "acts of God" in life. Disasters are the natural boomerang effect of the collective negativity that was being emitted, absorbed by nature, and returned.

The more you know about you and why, the more you can understand you and work to make the changes to a better you!

Listen to Your Words

How many people really listen to the words they speak? How many people realize the power of the spoken word? The spoken word can lift people up or tear them down. The same is true for us; we put ourselves down without ever realizing the damage being done.

What you think, believe, speak, and feel, you create. The more you believe in a thought, the more emotion you put into it, the more you create the outcome.

We all came to this school called Earth to be co-creators with God. We came to expand the Light and Love of the world. Your I AM Presence (that spark of God living within you) and God (the Great I AM) work together to create your world through thought. When thoughts are negative, the result is fear; when thoughts are positive, the result is love.

When we use the words, "I am," we call on God, the Great I Am, to help us create the word immediately following "I am." In other words, when you say, "I am poor," you are calling on God to create a situation of poverty. When you say, "I am sick," you are calling on God to create an illness within you. When you say the words, "I am," you are making a statement about who you really are.

One other word to watch is the word "need." "Need" equals "lack" equals "lessons." In other words, when we say we need someone or something, we believe there is a lack within us, which means there will be a lesson to show us we have everything we will ever need.

Listen to your words. How often do you say the words "I am?" Is the word immediately following positive or negative? Your world was created through thought; your words and actions validate your thoughts. What kind of world are you creating?

Listen to your words when it comes to your health. Once you put a name to your dis-ease, you own it. We say, "I have ...." How easy is it to get rid of something you have? We all have things we don't need in our homes, but how often do we clear it out? As long as you are saying, "I have …," you will not get rid of it. Instead say, "I Am releasing now whatever caused … within my being now, going back to the root wherever it started. I Am healing all of my bodies now." Ask for healing to go to the root, because the root most likely is not in this lifetime. From my past-life regressions I have learned most problems experienced today began in a past life. Heal the past to heal the present!

Listen to the words you say to others. Before speaking, ask: "Is what I am about to say true?" "Is it necessary?" and "Is it kind?" Remember, it's not what you say but how you say it that counts. Unspoken words can sometimes be more powerful than spoken words. Choose your battles. Timing is everything.

Use Your Mirrors!

Everyone and everything in life is a reflection of some aspect of you—positive or negative. The Law of Reflection allows us to see ourselves in the reflection of others. In order to move forward on your spiritual path, you must take time to look. Use your mirrors to see what is really going on within you.

When you feel it in your gut, it's your stuff (fear). It is a warning that something is not right. When you feel it in your heart, it's right (love). Full speed ahead! What you don't like in someone else is something you are either doing, have done in the past (past lives included), or you are capable of doing. Either way, it is a reflection of you. Take time to look into the mirror!

Take time to look at the signs. When change takes place, we feel an uncomfortableness that we can't explain. A certain area in our life becomes challenging (such as work or marriage). Because we have trouble accepting change, life will become temporarily difficult to push us where we need to go.

The **physical body** is a mirror to show us what is going on within. Negative thoughts and emotions and false beliefs come back in the way of life lessons or dis-ease. We can lie to ourselves about our feelings and emotions, but our body never lies.

Fear creates tension, which constricts or blocks the flow in the body, allowing dis-ease or illness to flourish. What we can't stomach in our life will show up as digestive issues. Change your way of thinking and you change your way of being.

If we say we want to do something, yet shift our eyes at the same time, we are not being truthful. If we cross our arms when someone is speaking to us, we are not comfortable with what is being said. Coughing can reflect resistance or it can be a way to get attention.

Slumping shoulders indicate someone low on energy or carrying "the weight of the world" on their shoulders. A stiff neck reflects a rigid way of thinking. A pain in the neck reflects someone who is our "pain in the neck."

The skin is our filter. Are we too thin-skinned or too thick-skinned? When we feel irritated, it will itch. What do we want to scratch? Rashes are the result of irritations over delays. When we burn or boil with rage, it will erupt with spots or boils or become inflamed.

Our eyes represent the way we see things in life. Eye problems represent what we don't like to see in our own life. What don't we want to see? If we are afraid of the future, we become near-sighted; far-sighted if we don't like what we see in the present.

We all hear what we want to hear, based on our belief system. So if we expect to be hurt and rejected, we unconsciously don't hear certain words or we imbue them with the hurt or rejection we expect. If we expect to fail, we read failure into what we hear.

We are tuned in to hearing what is important to us. That is why we selectively hear our name mentioned in a crowded room. If we give ourselves an earache, we don't like what we hear. People with nagging or overly talkative partners sometimes withdraw into deafness. The deaf ear is often the side is where their partner sits.

When we have ongoing fears and hurts, we protect the channels of our bodies with walls. So we harden our arteries. The additional weight around our mid-section is a wall we put up to keep from getting hurt.

Deeply held fears are buried more deeply within our bodies. We bury these fears and negative feelings in our livers, kidneys, or gall bladders.

Of course, our bodily health is also affected by the physical. We eat the way we feel. To stay healthy we must eat healthy foods, get enough exercise, and maintain a peaceful environment with enough stimulation and interest to keep us alert.

When our minds are clear and in tune with all of our bodies, we automatically choose what is best for us mentally, physically, spiritually, and emotionally.

The more sensitive we become, the more open we are to other people's feelings and emotions; the more likely we are to pick up another's pain and illness.

A true empath will be able to feel someone's pain, and then let it go. If the empath cannot let go of the pain right away, they are connecting with their own dormant emotions, which need to be resolved.

It is easy to lie to yourself, but your body will never lie to you. Take time to look at your reflection in the mirror to make the necessary adjustments on your path to becoming a better you. Your world begins and ends with you.

Everything in Life is Symbolic

Everything that is around us is symbolic of what is going on inside us. Our car, our home, our garden, our animals, our friends are all reflecting parts of ourselves. Describe any one of them, and you describe an aspect of yourself.

Your **house and car** represent you and how you represent yourself to the world. Describe them and you describe yourself. How clean do you keep your car? Your house? Where is your clutter? Each room in your house represents a different relationship with yourself and others. Your car represents your physical body.

The outside of your house represents what you want the world to see about you, while the inside of your house represents your inner thoughts. Do you have flowers (positive thoughts) in your garden, or do you have weeds (negative thoughts) in your garden, which can get out of control?

The family room represents your relationship with your family. The kitchen represents your ability to create with love. A clean kitchen and a light over the stove help to keep the creative juices flowing. The basement represents things from the past stored deep within us. Your bedroom represents your soul.

Fires represent "burning" anger deep within. Backed-up pipes represent emotions backed-up within you. A flood represents overflowing emotions.

A speeding ticket represents the need to slow down in life. Accidents are a sign your world is "crashing" in on you. When you get "lost" driving somewhere, where have you lost your direction in life? Where have you taken a "wrong" turn in life?

Our **pets** can be a mirror back to us. Animals can take on our characteristics. They learn by example. Loving pets have loving owners; needy pets have needy owners. Pets without boundaries have owners without boundaries. Spoiled pets have owners who like to be spoiled.

Sometimes our pets love us so much they take on our dis-ease so we don't get sick. What dis-ease do they have? Every dis-ease is symbolic of what is going on with you. What do you need to look at?

Nature can be a mirror back to us, individually and collectively. Bug bites represent areas in our life where we feel guilty over small things that "bug" us. Losing power in a storm represents feeling powerless in life. Lightning and thunder break up negative energy. Rain washes away the tears. Winds bring about change.

Has a bird or animal come to you in a most unique way? This, too, may be a mirror. The hawk and owl are messengers. Robins and cardinals represent new growth coming in. Raccoons represent someone pretending to be something they're not.

Dreams can also be messages about our lives. Some may be a symbolic message, and some may be a warning. Dreams can reflect our fears (nightmare) or a way to release the stress and emotions of the day.

126

No matter where we go in life, no matter what we do, we cannot escape ourselves. Moving away from a job or city won't guarantee the lesson is left behind. It will follow you wherever you go because it is a lesson you chose to learn. Learn the lesson so it won't have to be repeated. Learn the lesson so you can move on to the next one.

Lesson 6

A Map for Success

"You've always had the power, my dear. You just had to learn it for yourself." ~ Glinda, the Good Witch, "The Wizard of Oz"

The following pearls of wisdom can help you move through life with ease and grace:

Life is a learning experience. We learn from our mistakes. We would not be in life today if we didn't have lessons to learn. There's no need to be perfect to inspire others. Let others be inspired by your imperfections.

Being rude doesn't take any effort at all. It is a sign of weakness and insecurity. Kindness shows great discipline and strong self-esteem. It is not always easy to be kind when dealing with rude people. A person who is kindhearted has done much personal work and has come to great self-understanding and wisdom. Choose to be kind over right and you'll be right every time, because kindness is a sign of strength.

Stay away from narrow-minded people. They will only bring you down. Have a vision and stay focused on it, regardless of obstacles encountered to succeed. Do not rely on your past accomplishments to get you through life. Keep looking for new areas to grow. Life will be much richer. People who achieve great things in life are not afraid of challenges. They relish them and use them to their advantage.

Whether it's your personal or professional life, always test the commitment of people with whom you want to share a relationship. Get out of your comfort zone; there is no growth there. Shed old habits and behavior patterns that no longer serve you. Anything that burdens you or adds no value to your life should be released.

Define yourself by the example of love you have become rather than the religion to which you belong. Love is what motivates the soul.

You'll never know what you can do or be until you do your inner work. Each day is a gift. Look for the blessing to find the gift. We all have our own unique gifts and talents; use them to benefit others.

Find your purpose by doing what makes your heart sing. Your heart will never steer you wrong. Being in service to others is the most rewarding thing you can ever do. Helping just one person might not change the world, but it could change the world for the person you helped.

We don't grow through the good times. We grow through adversity. Have faith and trust in the process of life. Keep an open mind or you will never know Truth.

The greatest stress you go through when dealing with a difficult person is not fueled by the words or actions of this person. It is fueled by your mind that gives their words actions and importance.

It's okay to be upset. It is never okay to be cruel. Rage,

resentment, jealousy, and envy do not change the hearts of others—they only change yours.

Release those who hurt you. You deserve peace. Releasing them frees you from being the eternal victim.

Bullies appear strong on the outside, but they are weak inside. What are they protecting? What don't they want you to see? Don't let anyone bully you.

Smile often and stay positive in the midst of negativity. It's an easy way to shift others and make a difference in the world.

Gossip and drama end when it reaches a wise person's ears. Be wise. Always seek to understand before you attempt to judge or put down others. There are always two sides to every story. The positive choices you make will help to build your own character.

Be an example for others to follow. Treat everyone with kindness and respect, especially those who are not nice to you. They are a reminder to you of what not to be.

Drama is a babyish way to get attention. The way we treat others is an example of our ability to love, have compassion, and be kind. Count your blessings, value the people who matter most, and move on from the drama with your head held high.

The positive changes you desire cannot take place if you surround yourself with negative people. It is too easy to become like them without even knowing it. Just because you are kind to someone does not mean you have to spend time with them.

If you really want to be happy and at peace, stop trying to be someone or something you are not. Stop caring about what others think of you. It will only destroy you. Help others to be who they truly are as well.

When you feed a man a fish, he eats for a day. When you teach a man to fish, he eats for the rest of his life. Help someone, but do not make them dependent on you or you will incur karma.

No man is an island. You cannot build a house without help. Don't be afraid to ask for help. We are to be interdependent in life, not so dependent on others that we can't live without them or so independent that we think we don't need anyone.

And remember, you cannot change people who don't want to change, but you can change the way you react to it. You cannot make people hear what they don't want to hear or see what they don't want to see. But you can change you. And when you change, your world will change with you.

> *"Be the change you wish to see in this world." ~ Mahatma Gandhi*[50]

Mastering the Self

We came to this school called Earth to experience all of the emotions. To graduate we must learn to master the emotions instead of allowing them master us. Learn to work from the heart and not the gut.

To master an emotion does not mean to ignore or bury it. To master an emotion means to respond (a heart response) rather than react (a gut reaction).

When we react, we either lash out verbally or get scared and say nothing at all, burying the emotion. Sooner or later these emotions must come out, and when they do, they usually take the form of an even stronger emotion—anger.

To respond, walk away, take a few deep breaths, review the situation thoroughly, look at things from all perspectives, and then respond in a calm, effective, productive way to bring peace to the situation.

Many people think being a peacemaker means remaining quiet, not ruffling any feathers. This is not true. Sometimes feathers have to be ruffled to bring about resolution. A true peacemaker works to find a suitable compromise for all parties to walk away content.

Many people are familiar with the story of Jesus walking on water, but most are not familiar with the symbolism behind it. Everything Jesus did was symbolic. Jesus taught many different people on many different levels. He used parables to get his message across. Jesus was a master teacher, and any good teacher will help you look at yourself to bring about change.

For example, when Jesus walked on water, one person may think "Look at him! He truly is the son of God because he walked on water." But Jesus also taught we were all sons and daughters of God and that what he could do, we can do. So why are we not doing our work? Where is our faith?

"I solemnly assure you, the man who has faith in me will do the works I do, and greater far than these." (John 14:12)[51]

Another person may think, "Look at the faith he has. He can walk on water!" But Jesus also taught:

"Because you have so little trust," he told them. "I assure you, if you had faith the size of a mustard seed,

you would be able to say to this mountain, 'Move from here to there,' and it would move. Nothing would be impossible for you." (Matthew 17:20)

Jesus was not talking about physical mountains. He was talking about the mountains we make out of molehills in our daily lives.

Jesus' walking on water was symbolic. Water represents the emotions. Jesus taught that if we do not learn to detach from our emotions, we will drown in them. Detaching does not mean we don't care. It means we want to see our way through.

Think of an electrocardiogram (EKG). This test monitors the electrical activity of the heart. The spikes and the dips in the line are referred to as waves. When it flat-lines, we are considered dead.

The EKG can also be compared to how we live our life. When the line spikes and dips, it represents the emotional roller coaster ride we live (up one minute, down the next). A flat line represents depression; no emotions are felt. We feel "dead" inside. When the line goes up and down ever so slightly, our life is in balance.

The emotions scream, "Yippee!" or "Oh, no!" The heart says, "Oh, isn't that wonderful!" or "It'll be all right."

When we wallow in the emotions of ego and fear, we are self-centered. When we work from the heart with compassion and love, we are other-centered.

Learn to master the emotions so they don't master you.

Loving the Self

You cannot truly love another until you can love yourself. Without respect, there is no love. So what does it mean to love yourself?

To love yourself means to be selfish, to take time for you. If you don't, no one else will. Selfishness and self-centeredness are two entirely different things. You want to be selfish, not self-centered.

Loving yourself means respecting the temple you created—the physical body, the vehicle in which your spirit resides.

Everything in life has a consciousness, but not everything has a spirit. The more you talk to your plants, your house, or your car—even your body—in a loving way, the better they will serve your every need. Talk to your body. Love your body. It will respond in the same way you respond to it.

To love you means to take time to pray and meditate; to respect your body by eating healthy, taking your vitamins and supplements, and exercising. We all need to be a little more selfish and a lot less self-centered.

To love you means to stop beating up on yourself. Treat yourself with kindness, tolerance, generosity, and compassion. Everyone has their challenges in life. You are not responsible for what others say or do to you, but you are responsible for how you handle you.

To love you means to stop being a "people pleaser," someone who "buys" love. "BUYING LOVE" is not "BEING LOVE." No matter how much love you receive, it will never be enough if you do not love yourself, for all true love comes from within.

Lesson 7

Attaining and Maintaining Prosperity

No matter how much we want prosperity in our life, we will never achieve it if we continue to hang on to outdated belief systems. There are three types of people:

- Those who have a good sense of self-worth and are able to attract prosperity
- Those who are able to attract prosperity but spend it as soon as it comes in (unconsciously they do not feel they are worthy), only to find themselves deep in debt
- Those who cannot even begin to attract prosperity

Money Equals Self-Worth

Our finances reflect our self-esteem and self-worth. Those with a poverty consciousness must work to release any vows and promises made in the past (past lives included), beliefs and behavior patterns which keep them from attaining prosperity. You will never be able to accumulate money until you begin to value yourself.

We always have what we need in life. We get into trouble when we want for more than we need.

Abundance is Our Birthright

The Law of the Circle plays a very important role in our prosperity. The give and take of our money must be balanced. In other words, if we receive more than we send out or vice versa, an imbalance is created that blocks the flow.

Man's fall from grace was a result of our own human self-centeredness. We had forgotten the agreements we originally made with God.

God provides us with everything we need to sustain life, and, in return, we must balance our gift of Life by working to increase the Light and Love in the world. This is done through expressions of love, decrees, gratitude, respect, wisdom, abundance, peace, joy, happiness, and anything that blesses all life on Earth.

Even though we receive and use the gifts of life God provides for us, we do not always give back. This self-centered behavior is what blocks the flow of God's abundance. We can release this poverty consciousness by doing what we agreed to do in the first place.

Increasing Cash Flow

Money is used as a means of balance, so to become prosperous, we must increase our flow of money. This can be done by applying the Universal Law of the Circle. What we send out in the form of energy will expand and return to us. Money is a form of energy. In order to attract more money into our lives, we need to send out more money to help others.

The key to increasing cash flow is to give a portion of our money to people or organizations that will use it to increase the Light and the Love of the world. Donate money to organizations, charities and spiritual groups, human- or animal-rights and environmental groups, the arts and education, or to any organization that is working to improve the quality life on this planet.

Donate as little as ten percent of our income in appreciation for our gift of life to receive the flow of God's immeasurable abundance.

The Attitude of Gratitude

The attitude of gratitude with which we give our money away is critical to our success. Money given away must be used to improve the quality of life on the planet. It must be freely given away with no strings attached, not even so much as a "thank you"; you will have received the balance.

When we reprogram ourselves to expect prosperity—and believe it will happen—money given out will return tenfold. There is no limit to the return we can expect.

Decreeing with deep feeling opens the door to receiving God's infinite abundance. Recite the following decree when you donate money to a charity or organization:

I AM donating [$10.00] to [Name], an organization that is working to increase the Light and Love of the world, and in return, I AM gratefully receiving [$100.00] on the return current.

Consciously expect to receive an increase of money. Focus on the end result. Feel how happy you will be when you receive this money. Do not limit God by trying to figure out where the money will come from; just be open to receive.

Each time we receive unexpected money or someone buys something for us or pays for something we thought we were going to have to pay for ourselves, accept this as God's abundance flowing back into our lives.

When we come across a sale or if our bills are less than we thought they were going to be, this is a gift of money coming back to us. If someone gives us an item we thought we were going to have to purchase or if we get a raise or a higher-paying job, we are receiving God's abundance. If someone finally pays an old debt that we thought was lost forever or we receive a bigger refund than we had expected to receive on our tax returns, acknowledge the money as part of our returning abundance. Always give gratitude for money received. The more you give gratitude for something, the more you will receive of it.

The giving and receiving of money with love and appreciation for our gift of life helps to be more aware of God's presence in our lives.

Believing is Everything!

Believe and have faith! Your capacity to create prosperity depends on your faith in yourself. If you do not believe prosperity is possible, it cannot happen. You are the creator of your world!

Lesson 8

How Will You Be Remembered?

I am not the same soul I was once. A lot has changed. A lot had to change. So don't expect out of me what I embodied in the past for that part of me no longer exists. ~ Author unknown

We all want to be remembered when we die. How will you be remembered by those who knew you?

What contribution(s) are you making to make the world a better place? How are you making a difference in people's lives? How are you growing as a spiritual being? It is easy to help those we already know, but the greatest reward comes from helping people we do not know.

We could have donated $1 million to an institution and gotten our name on a plaque or a wing named after us, yet it matters not when we go Home. We could have run a large international corporation or gained great wealth, yet it matters not. We could have been an Olympic champion or famous sports figure, yet it matters not. The only thing that matters when we go Home is what we have become as a result of our many experiences in life.

People who receive accolades and rewards while in life do not receive them when they go Home. There is no "double-dipping." The dharma or grace we receive when we go Home as a result something we said or did with no thought of remuneration is greater than anything we could ever receive in life. If we have to tell someone what we did, we have already received our reward. It's called "attention."

Dharma comes from the little things we do, like helping to shift someone so their day can get better. For example, the clerk at the grocery store has a frown on her face, and you say something nice to her to make her smile, "I really like your outfit" or "That color looks good on you." In doing this, you shift her state of being and help her to smile.

> *"Not all of us can do great things. But we can do small things with great love."* ~ Mother Teresa[52]

Service is a way of life, and when the love you once gave out comes back to you, it is the most amazing feeling!

The best way to be remembered is by supporting causes that are important to you or by helping to transform and heal someone's life. Reach out and touch the lives of people you don't know. Share your blessings with others. Be a mentor to someone who needs it.

What are you passionate about? Your passion can become your legacy. How will you touch other people's lives? This is how you will be remembered.

Will the legacy you leave behind be positive or negative? The choice is always yours.

Blessings to you on your journey through life!

APPENDIX

Tools to Use on Your Journey through Life

"Remember, when you are making upward
spiritual progress, lower portions of the universe
will make attempts to bring you down."
~ Source/God through Elliott Eli Jackson

Life is fair when we understand how it works. Life does not have to be difficult. We make it difficult when we listen to the ego (Edging God Out) instead of our inner guidance, and what we resist persists.

Life is a process. We hear people say: "Two steps forward, one step backward." Rushing the process never works. If we skip a step along the way, we will go back to learn it. Do not try to force life. Everything takes place in Divine Timing, and Divine Timing is always perfect!

To bake a cake, one must have all the ingredients. If you leave one of the ingredients out, the cake will fail. When the batter is ready, it is put into pans to bake in the oven. If pulled out too soon, the cake falls. If left in too long, it burns. Having all of the ingredients and perfect timing are crucial for a successful outcome.

The body is a finely-tuned instrument. When one body is out

of alignment, they are all out of alignment. When we take unnecessary supplements and medication, we throw off the chemistry of the physical body. For example, too much or too little oil in a car or fluid in the transmission can break a car down. Putting water in the gas tank will do the same.

If we love ourselves, every day we will:

- take time for prayer (talk to God)
- meditate (10 minutes every day)
- eat healthy (eat organic whenever possible)
- take the necessary vitamins and supplements (muscle test to know what your body needs and the correct dosage)
- exercise (15-30 minutes, 2-3 times a week, depending on your ability)

If we do not love ourselves enough to take time for us, no one else will. Synchronicity takes place when all our bodies are in sync and our vibration is high. And when we are in alignment, magic, mystery, and miracles take place!

We can live a life with ease and grace...and learn our lessons at the same time. It's all in how we handle life. Everything happens for a reason and a purpose. This book came to you because you were ready for change. By changing your beliefs and your attitude, the world around you will change, too—for the better!

The following tools can help you to live a life with ease and grace. And, as I remind all my students often, tools are no good if you don't use them! Blessings to you on your journey!

Tools for Health and Healing

*"Health does not always come in the form of
medicine. Most of it comes from peace of mind,
peace in the heart, peace of soul. It comes
from laughter and love." ~ Anonymous*

Acid vs. Alkaline

Cancer cells cannot grow and disease cannot exist in a high alkaline body. The body stays strong when pH is maintained. Spiritually thinking, alkaline is symbolic of love and acid is symbolic of fear.

Normal pH is 7.0–7.4. The ideal pH level is 7.4 or higher so all the functions of the body perform effortlessly. Test strips (available at most pharmacies), also known as litmus paper, provide an inexpensive way to monitor pH levels. To use the test strips, place a small amount of saliva or urine on the strip and wait for the color to change. Compare the pH color on the strip with the pH color on the box to find your pH number.

If your body's pH is low, you are probably low on minerals such as sodium, potassium, magnesium, and calcium.[53]

A diet of 80 percent alkaline- and 20 percent acid-forming foods is recommended to maintain proper balance.

Breathe!

For a more joyous outlook on life and to calm the emotions, take time to breathe. Breathe in the breath of God using deep breaths at least twice a day.

Empty the lungs of stale breath. Form the mouth into an "oo" sound and breathe out heavily. Stand erect, with your feet together and your arms resting at your sides.

- Slowly inhale (filling the diaphragm) to the count of five, raising your arms over your head. As you inhale, push the diaphragm out.
- Hold to the count of five while visualizing a shaft of Golden White Light pouring down from your crown chakra and going through every part of your body and into your energy field.
- Exhale to the count of five, slowly lowering the arms back down to the sides.
- Hold to the count of five.

Repeat this seven times. This is a great way to release stress and bring you back into balance.

Crystals

About Crystals

Crystals have been used to assist in the healing process for thousands of years. They have been mentioned in the Bible. The high priest Aaron used them in his breastplate to communicate with angels. King Solomon's ring (gemstone) gave him power over the elements.

Throughout history, precious and semi-precious stones (crystals) were used in the crowns of kings and queens and in the statues of gods and goddesses, symbolizing their association with mystical powers. The diamond is used in wedding bands today as a symbol of purity.

Crystals are energy transmitters. They can absorb, focus, and transmit subtle electromagnetic energy; for example, watches and radios use quartz crystals. For this reason, they make excellent healing tools. Because crystals have a pure energy that vibrates at a fixed, stable, and unchangeable frequency, they can bring our energy level to their energy level. Upon coming into contact with a crystal, the vibrations of the crystal will interact with and change your vibration, bringing you back into a state of peace and harmony.

Crystals are used today in clocks, radios, microwaves, computers, and much more. There was resurgence in the use of crystals in the 1980s and 1990s. Interest in crystals grew and made headlines in newspapers, magazines, and television shows.

The human body cannot exist without minerals. Minerals can grow into crystals if they have enough space. Quite often there are so many different crystals growing in the same little space that none of the crystals are able to grow very large. The physical body can receive minerals from the crystal by placing the crystal on the body.

Resonance is the key principal of crystal healing. Since most matter is crystalline in nature, our bodies take on the energy being transmitted from the crystal. Quartz crystals have a similar molecular structure to water, which responds when charged with crystal energy by developing a more coherent crystalline structure. Since our bodies are mostly water, healing intentions directed and amplified through crystals can easily transfer to our bodies and stabilize our health.

Crystals can be used in many ways: for healing, meditation, protection, and manifestation, to name a few. They can be used as an elixir and to improve the health of plants and an aura.

Now that you know the basic principles behind charging crystals, their creative uses are limited only by your imagination and clarity of intent.

Crystal Basics

Place crystals under your bed to help you remember your dreams or to facilitate restful sleep (especially amethyst), over doorways and windows for protection, in the office for efficiency and productivity. They can also be carried in pockets or purses.

To open the heart, carry a rose quartz. To heal a broken heart, carry a black tourmaline to remove negative energy.

Clear quartz is an amplifier. It is the most popular crystal because its many geometric configurations can be used for many different purposes.

Amethyst is considered a powerful yet gentle master healer to transmute negative energy and facilitate cooperation, protection, and balance during times of transition.

Fluorite and pyrite stabilize the thinking process and can help with studying or doing mental work over long periods of time. Students should carry this stone with them during test time and also wear something yellow to easily connect with knowledge.

Wear a black tourmaline to ward off negativity. Morganite and kunzite help to absorb negativity.

Other popular crystals that help to reduce stress include citrine, hematite, malachite, smoky quartz, and turquoise.

Drink plenty of water after a healing session to flush out the toxins.

To learn more about crystals, my favorite authors include:

Katrina Raphaell, Melody, Judy Hall, Ken Harsch, Naisha Ahsian and Robert Simmons.

Cleansing Crystals

There are many ways to clear crystals. One way is by washing them with fresh (river, stream, or waterfall) or tap water to remove negative ions. A soft toothbrush can be used to clean crystal clusters. Crystals with a hardness of 4 or higher or made of salt (selenite, for example) should never set in water or they will dissolve. When in doubt, do not use water.

Set them in a bowl or pan of water with some Epsom or sea salt. Leave them there for 1-3 hours. Rinse them off.

Sound therapy can be used to clear crystals; e.g., crystal singing bowls, tuning forks, and Tibetan bells. The sound emitted must be of a higher frequency than the stone you are trying to cleanse.

Smudge crystals using cedar, bury them in the earth for 1-3 weeks, or bury them in sea salt to release negative ions. Do not use salt with porous, water- or metal-based crystals such as opal, lapis lazuli, malachite, or hematite. When in doubt, do not use salt.

Reiki energy can also be used to clear and charge crystals.

Some crystals, like citrine and kyanite, never need clearing.

Charging Crystals

Crystals are like batteries. The more you use them, the more their energy is depleted.

There are many ways to charge or re-energize crystals. Use nature by placing them outside in a safe place. Use sunlight to break down the negative ions and to re-energize them. To charge crystals for meditation or dream work, place them in moonlight.

Some crystals fade in sunlight, such as amethyst, kunzite. Never let them sit in sunlight for more than one-half hour at a time.

Place smaller crystals in a large cluster of crystals, such as quartz or amethyst, to cleanse and charge them.

Gridding with Crystals

The following are notes from a workshop taken years ago with Naisha Ahsian, co-author of the book, *The Book of Stones, Who They Are and What They Teach*:

A grid is a geometric form created from stones that have the geometry of the overall geometric form; e.g., quartz is hexagonal (6-sided) in its structure. An array is the way in which the crystals are laid out. Clear quartz and candle quartz work best to grid a room.

When creating a grid, use stones that have the same geometric form of the overall grid you plan to create. This creates a coherency because the overall form mimics the actual geometric sacred geometry of the crystal itself, creating a more cohesive energy within the grid itself. For example, use six 6-sided stones when creating a hexagon-shaped grid. The termination of the stone is considered the seventh point. When you sit in the center of that grid, you become the seventh point, the termination of the crystal grid. When tested with an electromagnetic meter, a discernably different frequency was noticed inside the grid than outside of the grid (as with crop circles).

Arrays are not constructed according to the geometrical structure of the stones; however, if you put an array inside a grid, the energy of the grid will be amplified. Arrays can be any combination of stones set in any formation. They can be used to bring in love and abundance, a deeper meditation experience, and more; however, there is no coherence in arrays because there are varying geometries, minerals, etc. going on within the set of stones. A grid will create the large coherent field, which will then amplify the energetic structure of the array placed within it.

The six stones in the grid must be activated to be resonant with each other. Sit with the stones and activate them through your heart, expanding your energy field (raising the volume) to incorporate all of the stones in the primary grid. Make sure all of the stones are activated so they work together. Activation is critical.

Once the stones are activated, the grid will remain coherent until a "louder" energy comes along. Everything that comes into the grid will be amplified by it. Do not build a grid around your computer or you will amplify the microwaves coming off of your computer instead of mitigating them. This is why you should not use quartz around your computer. Quartz crystals are amplifiers. They easily resonate with microwave radiation and will amplify that microwave radiation. Do not use magnets around your computer or you can wipe it clean.

When gridding a room, size does matter. Use a larger crystal (approximately 6 inches in length) for a larger room and smaller crystals for a smaller room. Try to keep them all roughly the same size. They do not need to be huge. If your stones are too large, they cannot resonate with the intention for the grid because large stones have a large inherent amplitude, so it will take longer to achieve your goal.

Intention is important. Your frequency needs to be loud enough to shift the stones to bring in your desired intention.

The direction of the stone does make a difference. A clockwise crystal grid will create a vortex of energy. Clockwise vortexes are electrical vortexes that send energy out into the atmosphere. Counterclockwise vortexes are magnetic vortexes that draw energy in from outside the grid to the center of the grid.

To send a prayer out into the world, create a clockwise or electrical vortex. To bring in something you would like to manifest (e.g., prosperity, love), create a counterclockwise or magnetic vortex.

To bring in healing, create an etheric grid by standing your stones with the termination pointing up. Set the crystals in little flower pots with sand (¾ full). Sand is quartz and therefore an amplifier. The crystals create a forcefield as opposed to a vortex.

Crystals pointing toward the center of the grid are similar to a magnetic vortex because you bring energy in from the outside and focus it toward the middle. Crystals pointing outward from the grid are similar to an electrical vortex because your intention is sent outward into the world.

To protect a building, property, or garden, use 6-inch lengths of ¾-inch copper tubing. Cut the top of the tubing with a hacksaw so there are four petals on one end of the pipe. Set your crystal upright inside the copper tubing. Copper is an amplifier. Create the hexagon grid by digging six holes around the perimeter of the building, property, or garden. Place the quartz in copper tubing in the ground. Cover with dirt it so it is buried.

A neutral vortex is important when gridding a house. An electrical vortex in a house will make it difficult to stay grounded. A magnetic vortex can make you feel depressed; it will be difficult to raise a vibration. A neutral vortex will create a forcefield around the space to mitigate any external energies coming in.

Cloudy stones are just as effective as clear stones. For healing purposes, a single- or double-terminated quartz point will work. The internal structure of the stone, not its appearance, makes a difference in the outcome. Double-terminated quartz crystals do not work well for creating vortexes. To create a vortex, single-terminated quartz crystals work better because the energy goes in one direction only.

The color of a stone can be an indicator of the mineral concentration within the stone. For instance, a deep purple amethyst has more iron and magnesium, which can enhance a healing session. Even though the color in stones like amethyst and kunzite can be bleached out by the sun, the minerals are still there.

A crystal within 4 feet of your body will create a resonant field that can go wherever needed. Crystals do not have to touch the skin. All stones have energy, and they all work. River rocks and stones from the earth are more powerful stones.

Place crystals under your healing table to create a grid for healing, but keep in mind the resonance will not be high enough to encompass the client. It is better to grid the overall room so whatever you have under your table is amplified by the grid to ensure a positive outcome.

Animals are more sensitive to electromagnetic fields, which is why they can sense changes within the earth. Some crystals have too much energy for them. Be aware of this when working with animals.

All crystals are minerals, but not all minerals are crystals.

Rocks are usually a balance of several different minerals. For example, granite has quartz, danburite, and other minerals. Crystals usually have one or two different minerals, while rocks may have more.

Simon and Shuster's *Guide to Rocks and Minerals* details the geometrical form, mineral content, etc. of a stone.

Healing with Crystals

Crystal healing works because of the principle of resonance. Most matter is crystalline in nature and will take on the energy transmitted via other crystals, such as quartz. Quartz crystals also have a similar molecular structure to water, which respond when charged with crystal energy by developing a more coherent crystalline structure. Since our bodies are mostly water, healing intentions directed and amplified through crystals can easily transfer to our bodies and stabilize our health.

Crystal Surgery is an intuitive art. Healing practitioners have become adept at using crystals like energetic scalpels to remove unwanted blocks and excess energy (as in migraines, fevers, headaches), or as energizers to add energy where needed. Healing takes place on the etheric body and automatically flows in the physical body. Crystal surgery is one of the very powerful healing methods used at White Dove Circle of Light and Love.

Crystal Remedies

Following are a few of the many healing remedies using crystals. Be sure to rinse the stones to clear and charge them when you are through with them.

For Protection from Negative Energy

Place a black tourmaline in your left pocket to ward off negative energy, and a rose quartz in your right pocket to send love. (We bring in with our left, and send out with our right.)

To Dispel Depression

Place a rose quartz in your left pocket to bring in love, and a black tourmaline in your right pocket to release negative thoughts and emotions.

To Drain the Sinuses

The sinuses are where we store the minor irritations in life, which is why so many people have sinus issues. We have 18-24 hours to release a negative emotion or we store it in the body.

To release these minor irritations, strategically place three citrine crystals on the head while lying down: one on the third eye (middle of the forehead, just above the eyebrows), one under the left eye on the cheek bone, and one under the right eye on the cheek bone. Close your eyes. Leave the stones in place for 10 minutes.

To Release a Headache or Migraine

Headaches and migraines signify the brain (our computer) is getting ready to shut down, usually the result of being stressed out or overthinking. Lie down and place a lepidolite in mica on the third eye. Leave it there for at least 30 minutes to clear and balance any negative or excess energy.

To Keep from Falling and to Release Vertigo

Vertigo and falling often are the result of unbalanced energy. Two similar-sized shiva linghams can help bring about balance by placing one stone in a pocket on one side of the body and the other stone in a pocket on the other side of your body. Carry them with you daily.

To Release Blockages, Swelling, Pain, etc.

Two stones that can release blockages, swelling, pain, etc., are a fluorite point and a Faden crystal. A fluorite point is a fluorite crystal with a shape similar to a quartz crystal. Its termination consists of six triangles coming to a point at the top. A Faden crystal has a milky white, tube-like line of growth running from edge to edge through a quartz crystal. It can also be the blue vein running through a kyanite crystal.

Place the fluorite point (termination pointing up) or Faden crystal over the afflicted area. Hold it there for three to five minutes. The pulsing sensation felt is the stone releasing. Visualize a platinum shield at the end of the termination to transmute the negative energy into positive energy.

If using a fluorite point, take the terminated end of the fluorite point and basket weave the energy of the stone into your energy field when you are through releasing. Fluorite has healing properties. The energy from the stone will help to heal the afflicted area more quickly.

To Bring in Prosperity

Carry a small citrine stone in your wallet or purse.

Dealing with Anxiety and Depression

How to prevent an anxiety attack:

Breathe deeply three to four times, in through your nose and out through your mouth.

Use the five senses of sight, hearing, touch, smell, and taste to help bring someone back to the present moment. Look around to find:

- 5 things you can see
- 4 things you can hear
- 3 things you can touch
- 2 things you can smell
- 1 thing you can taste

This type of grounding can help when you feel like you've gone too far in your head and lost control of your surroundings.

Thump the thymus to help center, focus, and balance.

To Dispel Depression

Anxiety and depression are also the result of low-vibration enti-ties. Clear the lower vibrations from your energy field and spirit body daily by reciting a mantra to release them. Protect yourself daily by reciting the Platinum Shield. *(See Tools for Protection: Releasing Low-Vibration Entities and The Platinum Shield)*

Recite the twenty I Am Decrees given to us from Source/God through Elliott Eli Jackson to help raise your vibration and to help you to remember who you really are. Saying them daily will help to become a better you. *(See Tools for Spiritual Growth: Decrees.)*

Smudge your house. *(See Tools for Protection, Space Clearing)*

Decorate with fresh eucalyptus. Low-vibration entities do not like eucalyptus! Diffuse eucalyptus or release essential oil (Young Living). Place a drop of eucalyptus oil on your crown chakra, your third eye, your throat chakra, your wrists, and the top of your feet to push away the low vibrations.

Refrain from drinking alcohol or using recreational drugs. This is so important because they attract lower vibrations. When you feel yourself becoming lightheaded ("getting high"), your spirit is going out and a low-vibration entity is coming in.

Never give your power away to anyone or anything!

Our diet is also a major contributing factor to the way we feel. Seven foods that could boost your serotonin: eggs, cheese, pineapples, tofu, salmon, nuts, and turkey.[54] Eat foods that ward off depression:[55]

- Sweet potatoes – rich in Vitamin B6. Low levels of B6 have been associated with symptoms of depression.
- Spinach – rich in tryptophan and folate. Tryptophan and folate increase serotonin levels in the brain. Serotonin is a neurotransmitter that helps us feel happy.
- Cashews – very rich in tryptophan. Eating two handfuls of cashews is the equivalent of one dose of Prozac.
- Berries – rich in polyphenols, an anti-inflammatory. Inflammation (unshed tears) has been linked to symptoms of depression.
- Avocados – this superfood is rich in tryptophan, folate, and omega-3. Omega-3 has been known to reduce inflammation in the body and regulates the brain's neurotransmitters.

Bananas, almonds, apples, watermelons, cherries, yogurt, beans, eggs, and meats also increase dopamine levels in the body. Decrease sugar and caffeine intake. Avoid processed foods and junk food, which can lower the amount of magnesium in your body. Eat mangoes, which are high in magnesium, to calm the nerves. Take a daily vitamin and a high dose of a quality magnesium supplement, if necessary. Get plenty of exercise and the proper amount of sleep. Decrease stress. Set a routine schedule allowing for plenty of time for work and relaxation.[56]

Drink herbal teas. Eat high-alkaline foods. Dis-ease cannot settle into a body that is 7.8 or higher in alkaline. Alkaline represents love; acid represents fear.

Spend three to five minutes giving gratitude to God to totally shift your way of thinking and being. Gratitude will lift your spirit, raise your vibration, and help you to see the many blessings of life.

Be in service to others. When we are in service to others, we are too busy to feel depressed. It raises our vibration, pushing low-vibration entities away.

Meditation, not medication! Meditate at least 10 minutes every day to keep the blues away and to find peace within. When there is chaos in your life, there is chaos within. When there is peace within, there is peace in your life.

Play uplifting music, Native American flute, or classical music. This high-vibrational music raises your vibration and the vibration of the room.

Find joy in life by choosing to make time for you. Take time to be in nature. There's beauty in nature. It will help to ground you. Surround yourself with beauty. Find the beauty in life and in you.

Use and/or diffuse Frankincense essential oil, a proven anti-depressant with no side effects, to help dispel depression. Use and/or diffuse uplifting therapeutic essential oils blended to raise your vibration. Modern Essentials guidebook recommends lavender, orange and lemon, or a grounding blend to dispel anxiety and lemon and frankincense to dispel depression.[57]

Place a rose quartz crystal in your left pocket to bring in love, and a black tourmaline in your right pocket to release negative thoughts and emotions. Wear a blue lace agate to help maintain a peaceful state of being.

Take a hot bath using a handful of Dead Sea salts and a few essentials oils; e.g., eucalyptus, lavender, rose, geranium, or jasmine.

Use all of these recommendations to make a powerful antidote to keep the blues away with no side effects except happiness and well-being.

Eating Organic

The USDA National Organic Program (NOP) defines organic as: "food produced by farmers who emphasize the use of renewable resources and the conservation of soil and water to enhance environmental quality for future generations. Organic meat, poultry, eggs, and dairy products come from animals that are given no antibiotics or growth hormones. Organic food is produced without using most conventional pesticides; fertilizers made with synthetic ingredients or sewage sludge; or ionizing radiation. Before a product can be labeled 'organic,' a government-approved certifier inspects the farm where the food is grown to make sure the farmer is following all the rules necessary to meet USDA organic standards.

Companies that handle or process organic food before it gets to your local supermarket or restaurant must be certified, too."[58]

A truly organic product will have a "100% Organic" logo on the packaging. "Organic" means the product is 95-99 percent organic, and "Made with Organic Ingredients" means the product is 70-94 percent organic.

According to an April 2012 AARP bulletin, to be able to tell if grocery store produce is truly organic, look at the Price Look Up (PLU) sticker. If the produce is organic, the code will contain five digits beginning with 9 (95023). Non-organic produce will only contain four digits (5023). A five-digit PLU beginning with 8 means the item is genetically modified (85023).[59]

When a product is labeled "Natural," harmful toxins may be used as ingredients. While the best place to get fresh produce is at a local farmer's market, it does not guarantee the produce was grown in an organic environment.

Essential Oils

Essential oils were one of the first medicines used by man. Egyptian and Chinese manuscripts show they have been used for thousands of years. They are mentioned in the Bible many times; the three Wise Men gave frankincense and myrrh to baby Jesus.

There are more than 200 references to aromatics, incense, and ointments throughout the Bible. Frankincense, myrrh, rosemary, cassia, and cinnamon essential oils were used for the anointing and healing of the sick.

Ancient Egyptians (4500 B.C.) used essential oils and aromatherapy for treating illness and performing rituals and religious ceremonies in temples and pyramids. Cedarwood, myrrh, and frankincense were and still are used in the embalming process.

Essential oils are created from the natural aromatic volatile liquids in plants (shrubs, flowers, trees, roots, bushes, and seeds). These liquids contain the life force of the plant. Pure, therapeutic-grade essential oils are best because they are distilled from plants. Anything less may not be effective and can, in some instances, be toxic. The purity of the oil and the therapeutic value will determine how they will work with your body.

According to Gary Young, "Thought equals frequency. Essential oils absorb our thoughts. They are registered in the oils as intent. Intent is directed energy. When you apply an intent-energized oil on your feet, they can saturate all of your cells within 60 seconds, stimulating creative thinking and pushing negative energy out of the cells, thus increasing the frequencies of the cells throughout the body. In that uplifted state, you can create a new desire to be better tomorrow. You have no limitations but those you choose to accept."[60]

Essential oils are used for aromatherapy, massage therapy, emotional health, personal care, nutritional supplements, household solutions, and much more. They have been used to kill harmful germs and to balance moods, lift spirits, and dispel negative emotions.

Young Living and doTerra are well-recognized therapeutic essential oils.

Exercise
According to the Centers for Disease Control and Prevention, regular exercise is important for maintaining a healthy weight and

for reducing the risk of cardiovascular disease. One way to release weight is by reducing calories and increasing physical activity.[61] Another way is to release the emotions that caused the weight gain in the first place. Use the Trauma Release *(See Appendix, Tools for Health and Well-Being)* or the Emotion Code to help release stuck emotions.

Moderate exercise includes walking fast for 15 minutes, going for a bike ride, or cleaning the house two to three days a week. A more vigorous form of exercise would include jogging, running, swimming, and most types of competitive sports. Energize yourself!

Do it for your heart. Do it for you!

Grounding

To be grounded means to be rooted in the Earth. To maintain balance, we must be connected to Source/God and all of the Divine through the crown chakra at the top of the head and connected to Mother Earth through the feet.

Grounding helps to stay centered and focused. It helps to bring the body and mind back into the present moment. Here are a few ways to ground:

- Walk barefooted or lie on the ground
- Go for a walk or hug a tree
- Take a shower or bath
- Wear or carry a black tourmaline crystal
- Use an essential oil that helps with grounding
- Take a deep, cleansing breath in through the nose. Hold to a count of ten. Exhale through the mouth.

- Say out loud, "I Am grounded within the earth. I Am grounded within the earth. I Am grounded within the earth. And so it is uttered, and so it is done. Gratitude."
- Picture red roots coming from your feet, legs, and tail bone. Visualize them going deep down into the core of Mother Earth where there is golden white Light. The roots drink of this Light and bring this Light back up through the roots, into the body, and up to the heart where the Light runs through your circulatory system to every part of the body.

Herbal Remedies

Herbs have played an important role in man's history. They have been used for cooking and medicinal purposes. Herbs found their way into linen closets because of their pleasant fragrances, and they were used to dye homespun fabrics and leather. Herb gardens were an essential part of pioneer homes.

As more and more people become aware of the dangers of synthetic drugs and medications, herbal remedies are on the rise. Home remedies using herbs are considerably cheaper than prescription medicines and rarely have any side effects. Herbs can be easily grown outside in a garden or inside in a flower pot.

Popular herbs to keep on hand are mint, chamomile, thyme, and lemon balm.

Mint, often used as a breath freshener, has been reported to help maintain a healthy digestive system and calm stomach aches. Ginger can help calm the stomach, ease the build-up of gases, and increase circulation.

Chamomile is perfect for relaxation and a good sleep; it can ease colic and anxiety issues. Thyme can help relieve stomach cramps due to gas build-up, and lemon balm has been used in the treatment of colds and the flu. Lemon balm can help to heal scrapes, minor cuts, and insect bites; it can also help with anxiety and insomnia.

Tiger balm, nutmeg oil, feverfew, passion flower, lemon balm, and peppermint oil work to help relieve headaches. Ginkgo biloba works to help improve circulation and reduce inflammation.

While most herbal remedies enhance the body's natural ability to heal through rebalancing and cleansing, there are some that can be dangerous when taken with synthetic medicine. Be sure to consult a knowledgeable practitioner before taking remedial herbs.

Herbal Teas

Herbal teas have been around for hundreds of years in Asia and are a natural healing drink that can be served hot or cold. There are sipping teas, and there are healing teas. Most teas have less caffeine than coffee. People are beginning to drink more teas like green tea, oolong tea, white tea, and black tea than coffee or soft drinks because of their medicinal purposes and pleasant flavor.

Traditional teas (such as green, black, white, and oolong teas) are made from the dried young leaves and leaf buds of the tea bush (Camelilia sinensis). Herbal teas are not made from the tea bush; they are made from an infusion of flowers, spices, herbs, leaves, seeds, bark, fruits, berries, spices, and plant roots.

Healing teas have medicinal properties that have been reported to cleanse and detoxify, alleviate pain, reduce fever, induce sweating, boost the immune system, fight infection, calm the stomach, fight cancer, ease spasms, support the heart and liver, cause vomiting, induce coughing to bring up phlegm, calm the nerves, help with insomnia, and much more. They work over a period of time.

Healing teas have been used in baths, as a poultice, and as a tincture. They can be a natural way to bring the body's internal systems back into balance.

"Live" Water vs. "Dead" Water

Mineral and spring water are considered "live" water because the life force of the water helps sustain our life force. Both contain electrolytes and other minerals that support all cellular functions.

Mineral water comes from a well or mineral spring and contains natural trace minerals important to maintaining well-being. The type of minerals in the water varies from region to region. Mineral water replaces minerals the body naturally loses through the day.

Spring water comes from underground aquifers. The water is clear and has been filtered by solid rock. It, too, contains natural minerals important to the body. Minerals improve the taste of the water.

Purified and distilled water are considered to be "dead" water because all contaminants have been removed, as well as electrolytes and minerals important to the body.

Purified water can come from any source of water, including spring, ground, or tap water. The EPA requires that it meet significantly higher filtration and purification standards than those for regular drinking water (such as tap water).

Distilled water is water that has been through a distillation process. It is ideal for applications where minerals can be counterproductive (for example, machinery and cleaning products). While distilled water is the cleanest bottled water readily available, it is not good for drinking because it pulls minerals out of the bloodstream and other parts of the body.

Muscle Testing

Muscle testing is used by chiropractors, acupuncturists, and energy practitioners to test the body. Anyone can use it. The body will never lie to you. Use it to learn what is good for your body and to get answers about your body. Use it to find out if a product is for your very best and highest good.

When you ask your body a yes-or-no question, it will respond one way for a "yes," and another way for a "no." The body will remain strong when the answer is "yes" and weaken when the answer is "no." Negative words or thoughts weaken our energy field.

The best way to muscle test is to close the eyes, the entrance to the soul and your inner guidance, to keep the mind from overriding and manipulating the answer.

Test to determine if a supplement is for your very best and highest good and what dosage you should take. For example, you may need vitamin C while treating the common cold, but you may not need it when you are well again. Muscle test to be sure the brand will be beneficial for you.

Muscle test to better understand what is causing pain or disease in the body. Muscle test to see if you are ready to release it and what you should do to release it. People begin to get better when they get sick and tired of being sick and tired. As long as we are getting something out of our dis-ease, we still need it; such as attention, identity (we do not know who we are without it), karma, etc.

You can test for anything; just be ready for the answer. It may not always be what you wanted it would be.

There are many different ways to muscle test. Two of the most common are:

Sway Test: Your body is a crystal that can be used as a pendulum. Stand straight with your eyes closed. The eyes are the entranceway to the soul. Your mind can manipulate the answer if your eyes are open. Ask your body to show you a "yes." Your body will most likely sway forward or backward. Ask your body to show you a "no." Your body will most likely sway the opposite direction. Now ask your question to find your answer. If you would like to know if a particular product is for your very best and highest good, hold it to your waist, then ask the question.

"O" Ring: Make a circle by putting your thumb and index finger together. Do the same with the other thumb and index finger, interlocking the two circles together. Ask your body to show you a "yes," then try to pull the circles apart. Ask your body to show you a "no," then try to pull the circles apart. The circles should break apart with one of the answers. You will know the difference between a "yes" and "no" answer.

Always ask your body to show you a "yes" and a "no" before starting. If you don't test the body first, the answer received most likely be reversed and you will not know this. The body typically pulls forward for a "yes" and backward for a "no." If your body pulls in the opposite directions, your polarity may be off because you are dehydrated. Drink a full glass of water, and then try again in five minutes.

Now ask your question to find your answer. Ask "would it be for my very best and highest good to..." Phrasing your question this way will not take away free will; you decide whether or not you should do something. Your body may not answer you if you ask, "should I..." because it takes away free will.

Make sure you are grounded (eat nuts or dark chocolate). If you still cannot get a good answer, check your belief system (you may not believe muscle testing is possible) or rephrase the question. For example, begin your question with "Would it be for my very best and highest good to..." You may have a belief out of alignment or you may be asking a question that takes away free will.

Processed Foods vs. Whole Foods

Processed foods are put through a "process," produced in a manufacturing plant, packaged, and then put on a shelf to be stored until ready to be eaten. They contain artificial ingredients (preservatives, oils, sweeteners, and flavors) to enhance taste and to prolong shelf life. Cooking time is minimal or none. Ingredients include chemicals and other unrecognizable names. If you can't pronounce an ingredient or you don't know what it is, you probably shouldn't be eating it.

Natural or whole foods are grown in orchards, gardens, or greenhouses. They are unprocessed, unrefined, and have a shorter shelf life because they have no artificial ingredients. They are full of vitamins, minerals, antioxidants, phytochemicals, and fiber your body needs to be healthy. The life force in plants helps sustain our life force. Cooking them takes more time, but they are good for the body and soul.

The main difference between the two is Love. Love cannot be found in processed foods (machine-made). The more one loves to cook, the greater the love put into the food (home-made). Love makes food taste better. Homemade food fuels the physical body, and the love put into making the food fuels the soul.

Raise Self-Esteem
A Gift to Help: Low-Esteem Blocker Kit
The following is an excerpt from *The Sapiential Discourses – Universal Wisdom, by All There Is, Was, and Ever Shall Be* through Elliott Eli Jackson, Chapter 1 – "The Self Revealed"):

"Put together a low self-esteem blocker kit. If you are prone to bouts of low self-esteem, do the following:

- Have a list of close friends, those people you can call or email quickly.
- Call or email the individuals on your list and ask them to give you at least seven good qualities about yourself. Explain to them what you are doing. And remember, true friends will not hesitate to assist you.
- Ask them also to email or mail the list to you so you can view it when you are feeling down.
- When you receive them, put them in your kit.
- Each time you receive or hear something positive

directed to you, from any source, write it down and place it in your kit also.

- Make some notes of the positive statements you received about yourself with the names of the people who said them on the notes. Hang them around your house—for example, in the bathroom, kitchen, or office.
- Make a list of ten positive personal affirmations and repeat them to yourself twice a day.

"We tell you, if you do these things, along with meditation, prayer, and faith, whenever and wherever lower-vibrational influences make attempts to interject negativity into the mental portion of your being, you will be able to counteract the attempts. This may seem simple, but everything involving the spirit/soul is. Everything involving the spirit/soul is connected to the spirits/souls of others and the spirit of the universe, which is us, the we!

"It is imperative to note that the concept of negativity is not natural. Remember, you are love! Unhappiness is not in your makeup. It has been created by the human mental and reinforced by the emotional." [62]

Release Stress

A few ways to release stress, especially in the workplace, are to:

- Play harp, flute, or classical music in the background—allow yourself to connect with the music to keep the flow of energy moving through you and to prevent energy from getting stuck
- Breathe—allow your soul to reconnect with the breath of God

- Meditate—take 5-10 minutes to clear your mind
- Take a break and stretch—take time to disconnect and re-center yourself
- Yoga

Self-Healing Techniques

There are times when we need help with healing and for this we should always seek help, but there are also techniques we can use to heal ourselves.

Creative Visualization

Close your eyes and visualize emerald green healing light coming in through your crown chakra, down into your head, and watch it go through every part of your body, down to your feet. The green light moves through each one of your chakras and out into your energy field. Hold that vision, watching the green healing light move through you to heal and re-energize every part of your being.

Close your eyes and visualize emerald green healing light coming into the afflicted body part. See the body part healed. Know it to be true. Do this as often as necessary.

Request Help from Angels and Guides

Before going to bed at night, ask your angels and spirit guides to take you to the Jade Temple for healing while you sleep.

Talk to Your Body

Everything in life has a consciousness, including your body. Talk to it. Tell it how grateful you are for all that it has done for you.

Apologize for any trauma you have stored in that body part. Tell the body part it is time to heal, and you wish to help with its healing. Allow yourself to release the stored trauma. See the body part fully healed. Believe the body part is healing so the healing can take place. Anything is possible. The sky's the limit!

Thump the Thymus

Thump your thymus to center yourself and bring you back into balance. The thymus is a spiritual organ. Many women, especially the elderly, instinctively know to do this when something in life takes their breath away. They do this involuntarily.

Trauma Release

Decide what you would like to release. Set your intention to release "everything from past lives, present life, and future lives, going back to the root wherever it started." Then place one hand across the forehead and the other hand across the back of the skull at the nape of the neck (base of the occipital bone). Hold your hands in place and bring up (remember) the trauma. Allow your body to release in whatever way it desires.

Your head may go in circles or rock back and forth (nurturing the inner child); lean to the left or lean to the right. The left side of the body represents the past; the right side, the current time. You may cry, or your body may twitch or tremble. Your head may go backwards (exasperation), or it may go down. The farther down the head goes, the more deeply rooted the trauma.

No matter what happens, keep your hands in place and allow the body to release. You will know you are done when you experience a deep, involuntary breath. If the breath is not deep, repeat again at a later time. You are not yet ready to release it all. Peel back the many layers so you can get to the core of the trauma.

You can also place two drops each of Young Living's Release essential oil into the palm of your hands, and then rub your hands together. Inhale deeply three times; release through the mouth. Now use the trauma release. Using Release essential oil will help to release whatever it is you no longer need.

You can perform this procedure on other people, including children.

Other Techniques

Other self-healing techniques include: the Emotional Freedom Technique (EFT), the Tapas Acupressure Technique (TAT), and the Emotion Code.

White Dove Circle of Light and Love in Springboro, Ohio, teaches these techniques. You can also search the internet for more information.

Take Time for You

As the saying goes, if you do not take time for you, no one else will.

Take time to pray and meditate. Take time to eat healthy and take any appropriate supplements (always muscle test to see what your body needs). Take time to exercise.

Take time for a stroll in the park, to smell the flowers, and to soak in the bathtub (using therapeutic essential oils). Take time for a manicure or a pedicure; better yet, let someone else do it for you. Take time for a game of golf or a day at the beach.

Take time to laugh; laughter is the best medicine. Laughter helps to release stress; it will prolong your life.

The Attitude of Gratitude

Gratitude is the highest form of prayer there is. Give gratitude in advance for what you would like to receive; it shows you have faith that your request will be granted.

To create more of what you want in life, give gratitude for what you have. Give gratitude for having the money to pay bills, to put food on the table and clothes on your back. Give gratitude for good health, good friends, and for those who love and accept you as you are. Give gratitude in advance for what you want to happen, such as healing.

Three to five minutes of gratitude can help shift a negative way of thinking into a positive one. It can turn a bad day into a good one.

Give gratitude for the many blessings received in life, especially those not recognized. And remember to give gratitude for the many lessons in life for they helped to create the beautiful person you are today.

We always have what we need. We get into trouble when we want for more than we need!

The Importance of a Good Cleanse

The human body should be purged periodically of the many chemicals and minerals for which it should have only trace, if any, amounts. An excess of toxins can slow down the mind, body, and spirit; it can inhibit well-being.

Fasting to cleanse the body should only be done on a limited basis (once or twice a year) for no more than three days. Anything more can be detrimental to your health. During this time, drink only water and eat only small portions of raw vegetables to cleanse the blood and to aid your digestive system by removing unnecessary particles that need to be removed.

The Importance of a Well-Balanced Diet

A well-balanced diet provides the energy needed to make it through the day. It consists of all the vitamins, minerals, and nutrients essential to maintain a healthy body. A well-balanced diet supports the cardiovascular and immune systems and assists in weight control. The overall benefit is the feeling of well-being.

Foods should be organic and fresh, free of chemicals and preservatives. Whole grains (not processed grains), beans, and nuts should be eaten. More fish, fowl, and lamb should be eaten than red meats. Leafy, green vegetables (raw or steamed) and fruits should be eaten daily.

Milk should be included for calcium and protein. Foods should be rich in Vitamins A, C, and E; selenium; potassium; and fiber. Fried foods and an overabundance of sugars and alcohol should be avoided.

A well-balanced diet provides all the vitamins and minerals, calcium and protein necessary to support healthy cells, organs, and muscle tissue. A strong, healthy body makes it difficult for dis-ease to settle in.

The Importance of Nutrition

The human body is comprised of ten complex systems, each performing a different function to regulate the body: skeletal, muscular, nervous, endocrine, cardiovascular, lymphatic, respiratory, digestive, urinary, and reproductive.

There are six basic elements that make up the physical body: carbon, nitrogen, hydrogen, calcium, oxygen, and phosphorus. Other elements (in miniscule amounts) include: sodium, magnesium, sulfur, zinc, copper, molybdenum, selenium, chlorine, iodine, fluorine, cobalt, iron, manganese, lead, lithium, aluminum, strontium, silicon, arsenic, bromine, and vanadium.

Nutrition means eating a healthy diet, full of the nutrients found in fruits and vegetables grown in fertile soil. Four essential nutrients that make up the cornerstones of a healthy diet that keep the physical body in balance and functioning well: water, carbohydrates, fat, and protein.

- Carbohydrates found in plant foods get converted into glucose, providing energy for the physical body.
- Excessive fats cause problems in the body, but a reasonable amount of fat is required to support growth and to provide energy.
- Proteins can be found in meat, fish, eggs, nuts, seeds, and dairy products. They support the muscles, tissues, skin, and major organs.

When we feel positive and loving, we eat healthily (fresh fruits and vegetables, beans, and whole grains). When we feel lousy and think negatively, we tend to eat poorly (fried foods, unnatural foods, and sweets).

The foods we choose to eat and how we prepare our food will determine how well they will be assimilated in the body. Natural foods contribute to optimum health and longevity of the body.

The Proper Amount of Hydration

The most common substance found on earth is water. Every living thing requires water to survive. The human body is made up of mostly water.

Water is important for the body for hydration and digestion, for our teeth and bones. Water is important to flush the body of chemicals, toxins, and other waste products it contains. It regulates body temperature and maintains cleanliness by excreting urine and other poisonous substances from the body. It serves as a lubricant for the body, aiding in chewing, swallowing, and moving solids through the body. Water is the best cure for most illnesses.

Because the human body is approximately 70 to 90 percent water, most people (unless dehydrated) only need to drink four to six cups a day or the body will become oversaturated. Floppy fat is a sign of too much water in the body. The body can only process so much at a time, fluid or solid.

Just as too little water can lead to dehydration, too much water can cause mineral depletion and other imbalances within the body. Too much water can dilute stomach acids, causing acid reflux, and agitate a hiatal hernia. Too much water combined with a high-fiber diet can lead to bloating, gas, and other digestive disorders.

Tools for Clearing and Protection

Cutting Cords of Attachment

While in the womb, the umbilical cord connects the developing fetus to its mother. Its function is to supply oxygen, deliver nutrients, and withdraw blood rich in carbon dioxide and depleted in nutrients to the fetus.[63]

An ethereal or etheric cord is an energetic cord in the spirit realm that connects one person to another. It is a way to tap into another's energy. Have you ever thought of a friend and then that person called you? A cord went out and your friend received your thought through the cord.

Etheric cords can be anywhere on your spirit body or energy field, although they are usually found in the solar plexus (stomach) area of the body. Cords between romantic partners are usually found in the sacral (between the hips) area of the body. Cords can strengthen over time. The more you connect with someone, the stronger the cord becomes. Energy flows in both directions. An ache or pain in the mid-section of the body (a back ache, for example) can be the result of a cord. Cut the cord!

Cords can suck your energy. We all have that friend who does all the talking while you do all the listening. Your energy becomes drained just listening to them! Energy is only flowing in one direction. Remove the cord so this person will stop draining your energy.

Cords can also be created to psychically attack someone. Someone intentionally tries to steal another's power, leaving them to feel physically, mentally, and emotionally drained. Cords must be removed to maintain health and well-being and clarity of mind.

To protect yourself from being corded into while talking with someone, try the following:

- When you notice your shoulders begin to slump and your mind begins to wander, end the conversation. Tell the person you are talking to you have to go to the bathroom. Wait 10 minutes to call them back. Usually what this person was talking about is no longer important. Unconsciously, this person's main reason for calling was to suck your energy because their energy level needed refueling. When you end the conversation, cut the cord.

- Bring your feet together, interlace your fingers and place them across your stomach, bring your elbows in. Hold this pose as long as necessary. By doing this, a protective shield is created so this person cannot tap into your energy.

To remove cords:

- Visualize a Platinum Flame. Pull the cord from you and place the end in the Platinum Flame to be transmuted. Then pull the cord from the person who corded into you and place it in the Platinum Flame. Put the entire cord into the Platinum Flame.

To release a loved one that has crossed over, an ex-lover or friend, write a Release Letter and burn it (purification) so both parties can move forward to the next stage of their evolutionary journey. Release any cords.

Release letters are important. They remove "the tie that binds" so you can both move forward on your evolutionary journey. *(See Tools for Spiritual Growth: Release Letters)*

Help with Challenging People and Situations

Life can be challenging from time to time, dealing with difficult people and situations. What the world needs more of is love. So why not send love to help ease a situation?!

Namaste!

The Sanskrit word "Namaste" means "May the Christ in me meet the Christ in you." It means "My soul honors your soul."

Close your eyes and picture the person involved in your mind's eye and say out loud or through thought, "Namaste!" You are asking this person to meet you on a higher level of love. They can't be mean to you. If they can't be nice, they'll stay away...and that's okay.

The Christ or Higher Self is pure unconditional love. It knows no fear or negativity. Use "Namaste" when you travel, shop, or go out to eat to attract helpful, pleasant people. Write the word on a piece of paper and place it in your suitcase. Set the intention for your luggage to arrive with you and without damage.

Wearing "Namaste" jewelry carries the energy of the word with you wherever you go.

Use the "Namaste" daily so life will flow with ease and grace.

Talk to Their Higher Self

If you would like to get your point across to someone who is closed-minded, picture the person in your mind's eye and state your case. Then ask—never demand—what you would like to achieve. To demand something of someone's higher self is to take away their free will. Never take away someone's free will! It is a misuse of energy and will create karma.

Always ask for the very best and highest good for all concerned. Then allow life to take place. Keep in mind, sometimes what you asked for was for your very best and highest good, even though it wasn't what you wanted. Trust that as times goes on, you will understand why.

Send Unconditional Love

The only thing that heals is love. Magenta is the color of pure unconditional love. It is nurturing and compassionate. Surrounding someone in Magenta Light helps to soften them so they will be more receptive to your request.

Surround yourself and your loved ones in Magenta Light daily to help keep low-vibration entities away. These fallen angels are taught by their leaders that nurturing and compassion are not good. They want only the wisdom and energy with White Light. They do not want that "touchy, feely stuff." It repels them.

Use it daily to clear spaces where low-vibration people live; for example, a crack house or a residence with someone that makes you feel uncomfortable. Over time, these low-vibration people will move out and loving tenants will move in. This is something I personally witnessed. After one month of visualizing the Magenta Light through a shady man living in a nearby house, he was gone. The new tenants moving in were a loving couple engaged to be married. It really does work!

Releasing Low Vibration Entities

Signs that you have an entity on you, draining your energy: exhaustion for no reason, depression, yawning all the time even though you slept well the night before, grumpy attitude, thinking/acting negatively (out of character), a stiff neck, an ache or pain that moves around body.

These low-vibration entities attach themselves to your weakest areas and along the "T" line of the back (neck, shoulders, and spine). Anxiety and depression, bipolar and schizophrenia are all signs of low-vibration entities. Be aware of your energy at all times!

A mantra using Young Living's Release essential oil to remove low-vibration entities:

Place two drops each of Release into the palm of your hands, and then rub your hands together. Take three deep breaths, breathing in through the nose and out through the mouth. Say out loud:

"In the Name of All There Is, Was, and Ever Shall Be, I command all lower vibrational portions of the universe that are within, on, and around me in any other measure than as assigned by the universe, even in trace amounts, to leave me now, to leave my aura, my energy field, my mental, and my emotional. I further command you to leave the land that this building is on and every crack and crevice of my abode, away from my finances, my ability to intake money and pay my bills, and away from my other, my parents, my children and grandchildren, their auras and energy field. And so it is uttered, and so it is done."

Know it is done. BELIEVE it is done!

If you feel you have one or more spirits (yes, you can have more than one!) on you or in your energy field, say out loud, as necessary:

"In the name of All There Is, Was, and Ever Shall Be, I command lower vibrational portions of the All that are within, on, and around me in any other measure other than that as naturally assigned by the universe to leave. I send you away to your proper place of existence, which is not on this person, in this home, or on this land. And so it is uttered, so it is done!"

BELIEVE it is done, and it shall be.

When finished, you may notice yourself taking a deep breath—a sign you have released them. You may feel "lighter." Recite either mantra daily to keep lower-vibrational spirits away. If your words get twisted or omitted while saying the mantra, this is the lower-vibrations affecting you. Repeat the mantra meaningfully until you can say it clearly.

Use the following method if you want to feel and release a low-vibration entity:

Visualize God's Divine Light and Love as a pool of White Light. Ask the low-vibrations to go to the Light.

If they do not go, command them to go by saying, "If there are any entities within, on, or around me that are not of the highest Light and Love, I COMMAND YOU in the Name of All that is Holy and Pure to present yourself to me now. You are not welcome here." If you cannot say "in the Name of All that is Holy and Pure" clearly, you have a low-vibration entity on you.

Wait a few seconds to get their attention, and then say, "If there are any entities within, on, or around me that are not of the highest Light and Love, I COMMAND YOU in the Name of All that is Holy and Pure to move to my left arm now. You are not welcome here."

Wait a few seconds to give them time to move to your left arm, and then say, "If there are any entities within, on, or around me that are not of the highest Light and Love, I COMMAND YOU in the Name of All that is Holy and Pure to move to my left hand now. You are not welcome here."

If there is an entity, you will feel its energy in your hand. It may feel heavy, moist, tingly, whatever. You will feel it.

Once you feel them in your hand, say again, "If there are any entities within, on, or around me that are not of the highest Light and Love, I COMMAND YOU in the Name of All that is Holy and Pure to move into this pool of God's White Light and Divine Love."

Shake them off into the pool of God's Divine Love and Light you created, putting your hand into the Light to shake them off.

If they do not go, peel them off and put them into the Light. Flood your body with Magenta Light from your head to your feet.

You may have to repeat this procedure several times if you feel you have more entities on you. It is not unusual to have many.

Other Methods

Smudge yourself or someone else from head to toe, front and back, with cedar to clear, followed by sage to seal and protect.

Put a drop of eucalyptus oil on the top of your head, third eye, throat, each wrist, and the tops of your feet to keep low vibration entities away. They really don't like this essential oil!

Space Clearing

Space clearing is an art practiced in many ancient cultures. Just as dust and dirt accumulates in your home physically, the same happens with someone else's energy on an energetic level. You may not see the "dust and dirt" of human emotions, but they do accumulate in the spirit realm. Clear them out periodically.

When you get up out of a chair, some of your energy is left behind. The more you sit in the chair, the more your energy collects in that chair. It becomes comfortable because it has your energy in it. The same goes for a favorite blanket, article of clothing, or side of bed. Bring a favorite blanket of yours with you when you travel. Sleep with it for a better night's rest. Hotel beds have many other people's energy in them. That why we don't always sleep well in them.

Clear your home at least once or twice a year, especially after a major trauma has taken place, such as death or divorce. It is also important to clear a house you have just moved into, especially if the house was in foreclosure. Estate jewelry or inherited items should always be cleared before using to release any unwanted energy.

Experiment with different ways to find what works best for you. Here are a few methods to space clear:

Candles: Candles invoke the energy of purification and inspiration. They help to release stress. Their aroma is uplifting.

Herbs: Fresh herbs such as sage, cedar, fir, eucalyptus, and lavender can be used to purify energy. To keep low-vibration entities away, decorate a room or house with fresh eucalyptus in every room.

Incense: Use a natural, high-quality incense to freshen the air and calm the energy of your space. Cedar incense helps to clear negative or stale energy.

Essential Oils: Diffuse lavender, eucalyptus, lemon, mint, lemongrass, or wild orange to clear a space while, at the same time, providing beautiful aromatherapy.

Music and Nature Sounds: Sounds can also clear the

energy of a space, our mood, and our well-being. Playing high-vibrational, classic, or Native American flute music can shift your energy to find peace within. Place a bird feeder outside of your home. The sound of birds chirping helps to clear negative energy. That's why there are so many birds around hospitals and care centers.

Tibetan Bells or Crystal Singing Bowls: These bowls not only clear energy, they bring a powerful healing quality for those in the room. Take a bell over your head to clear you.

Crystals: Crystals can raise the vibration of a room while strengthening your own energy.

Fresh Flowers: Flowers are of a high vibration and can bring the energy of beauty, harmony, and joyfulness to any space.

Smudging

Smudging a home is always a good idea to clear stale or negative energy and low-vibration entities. You can also smudge a person or an item. The term "smudging" comes from the Native American shamanic traditions of clearing energy, although every culture has its own way of smudging. Smudging helps strengthen well-being. The smoke from the herbs unleashes the healing energy of the plant to neutralize and purify any negative presence.

When smudging, it is best to use cedar for clearing and sage to seal and protect. In olden days, a handful of cedar was thrown into the fire or onto a wood stove to clear the energy and musty smells in the room.

Place the dried cedar in an abalone shell or fireproof pan. Light the cedar so it begins to burn. Once the fire gets going, blow it out. It is the smoke you want because smoke goes everywhere. Using a feather or your hand, take the smoke around the outside of the house first, then the inside.

Inside the house, smudge each room, including closets, bathrooms, and basements. Open drawers, cabinets, appliances, etc. Send around doors, windows, mirrors, computer monitors and television screens.

Test to see if the room is clear by using a bell. If it is clear, the sound will bounce around the room and the tone will vibrate longer with each ring. Ring the bell over your head to bring you back into balance.

Once the rooms are clear, use sage in the same way to seal and protect the space.

The Platinum Shield

The Platinum Shield is a seal, a cover, a protection. In order to call this universal shield upon oneself, do the following:

- Center yourself
- Take a deep breath
- Exclaim the following from your being – Out Loud!

In the name of All There Is, Was and Ever Shall Be,
I call upon the universal Platinum Shield of Light.
I call upon the Platinum Shield to come upon my very being.
I call upon the Platinum Shield to cover me.
I call upon the Platinum Shield to protect me.

I call upon the Platinum Shield to hover over and around me.

I call upon the Platinum Shield to stand beside me.

I call upon the Platinum Shield to hold me up from my base.

I fully acknowledge the need for my shield's presence in my life now.

I fully recognize my shield's power as given to it from the Source of all things.

Mighty Platinum Shield, cover me from head to toe.

Shield me from all that is not in my highest good.

Protect me from disease, stress, worry and pain.

Shield me from all my personal addictions, for I do have some.

Shield me from those things that I need not be exposed to.

Come upon me in a mighty way,

Charge through my being,

Push away from me all that should not be in or around my being,

Let your power enfold me.

Send away from me all negative aspects of our great universes,

Intensely protect me.

From the power within me that comes from Source/God, I call thee.

I need thee, my shield,

Source/God has given you unto me – Come!

Protect me from all darkness,

Keep me in light and love.

Keep the darkness of my species away from me and mine.

Shoot in all directions from my being,

Protect those in my bloodline,

Protect those that are of a high vibration like me, seeking peace on Earth.

Platinum Shield be placed upon my chest,

Protect my heart of hearts,

Protect my soul.

Shield my mental from low thoughts and my being from low actions.

Cover me.

So it is uttered – So it is done!

Perfection I AM. Perfection I will be!

Now my Shield protects me.

This tool WE give unto thee. It is for the use of woman and mankind. Remember WE love you! ~ Source/God through Elliott Eli Jackson

Tools for Spiritual Growth

Beauty Raises Energy

Just in case no one told you today, you
are good enough. ~ Anonymous

Surround yourself with Beauty! It will uplift your spirit and raise your vibration.

Everyone loves to be surrounded by beauty, e.g., beautiful clothes, jewelry, artwork, flowers, music. Surround yourself with nature. Treat yourself to expensive candles, or play beautiful, soothing music. Place crystals in different rooms of your house. Diffuse essential oils. Make your surroundings at home and work more beautiful and radiant. A few small, inexpensive things can make a big difference in the way you feel.

Do something for yourself that inspires beauty. Drink tea out of a beautiful china cup with a silver spoon. Eat dinner by candlelight to create mystery and ambiance. A simple vase of flowers can be uplifting; the aromatherapy alone is soothing and healing. Put sachets in your closets and drawers so your clothes always smell good. Use incense or diffuse essential oils. Dance!

Everyone loves to feel beautiful. Buy a new outfit that makes you feel good or get a makeover. Wear a perfume that smells beautiful. Get your hair done, a massage or a Reiki session, a manicure, or a pedicure. Take a bath with essential oils and sea salts for a relaxing end of the day.

True beauty comes from within. When you feel beautiful inside, everyone else will see the beauty in you on the outside as well!

Codes of Conduct for a Disciple of the Holy Spirit

The following discourse is from the Maha Chohan (Great Divine Director) as written in *The Ascension Flame of Purification and Immortality* by Aurelia Louise Jones:[64]

- Become conscious always of your aspiration to embody the full expression of Godhood, and devote all of thy being and thy service to that end.
- Learn the lessons of harmlessness; neither by word nor thought, nor feeling will you ever inflict evil upon any part of Life. Know that action and physical violence will keep you in the realm of pain, suffering, and mortality.
- Stir not a brother's sea of emotion thoughtlessly or deliberately. Know the storm in which you would place his spirit will sooner or later flow upon the banks of your own life stream. Rather bring always tranquility, love, harmony, and peace to all life.
- Disassociate yourself from the personal and planetary delusion. Never allow yourself to love your little self more than the harmony of the universe. If you are right, there is no need to acclaim it. If you are wrong, apologize.
- Walk gently upon the Earth and through the universe, knowing that the body is a sacred temple, in which dwells the Holy Spirit, bringing peace and illumination to life everywhere. Keep your temple always in a respectful and purified manner, as befitting the habitation of the Spirit of Love and Truth. Respect and honor with gentle dignity all other temples, knowing that often within a crude exterior burns a great light.

- In the presence of Nature, absorb the beauties and gifts of Her kingdoms in gentle gratitude. Do not desecrate Her by vile thoughts, sounds, or emotions, or by physical acts that despoil Her virgin beauty. Honor the Earth, "the Mother" that is hosting your evolutionary pathway.

- Do not form nor offer opinions unless invited to do so, and then, only after prayer and silent invocation for guidance. Speak when God chooses to say something through you. At other times it is best to speak little, or to remain peacefully silent.

- Let your heart sing a song of gratitude and joy unto God. Be grateful always for all that you have received and that you have in the now moment. Tap in to the River of Life, River of Love and Abundance that lies within the Sacred Heart.

- In speech and action be gentle, but with the dignity that always accompanies the Presence of the living God that lives within the temple of your being. Constantly place all the faculties of your being and all the inner unfoldment of your nature at the feet of the God-power, endeavoring to manifest the perfection of compassion when meeting those in distress.

- Let your word be spoken in gentleness, humility, and loving service. Do not allow the impression of humility to be mistaken for lethargy, for the servant of the Lord, like the sun in the heavens, is eternally vigilant and constantly outpouring the gifts of Love to those who open their hearts to receive them.

Decrees

Affirmations work to create a condition or modify a behavior as long as the belief is in agreement with the affirmation. When the two are not in agreement, we stop saying the affirmation, thus stopping the process.

Decrees are more powerful because we call on God, the Great I AM, to help create a condition or modify our behavior. A decree always begins with the words "I Am."

Source/God has given mankind a discourse of Great I Am decrees that, "if stated and followed without prejudices, along with an open-mind, will change the claimer's life and the direction of your world."[65]

Following is an excerpt from *The Sapiential Discourses – Universal Wisdom Book III, by All There Is, Was, and Ever Shall Be* through Elliott Eli Jackson, Chapter 1 – The Great I AM, "Mankind's I Am Decrees" section:

1. I Am, You Are, WE are One

I AM one with all things. I AM one with God. I AM God in human form. I AM one with all humans and all humans are one with God. I AM one with the Earth on which I dwell. I AM one with all portions of Earth—the air, the water, the fire, and the wind. I AM the air, the water, the fire, and the wind. I AM one with all animals and sea dwellers. I AM one with all portions of Earth. I AM one with the oceans; I AM the oceans. I AM one with the rivers; I AM the rivers. I AM one with the mountains and the hills; I AM the mountains and the hills. I AM one with the grass and the dew; I AM the grass and the dew. I AM one with the rain and the snow; I AM the rain and the snow. I AM one with everything and everyone. I AM everything and everyone. I AM and can never be separate from self, from God. I AM divine. I AM eternal. I AM everlasting spirit, everlasting soul. I AM from the beginning to the end. I AM that which I AM and can be nothing else. So it is uttered, so it is.

2. I AM Perfect

I AM amongst the perfect ones. I AM perfect just as I AM. At each stage of my life I was perfect—seven perfect systems in synchronization with everything everywhere. I AM majestic. I AM regal. I AM powerful. I AM able to achieve that which I desire. I AM beautiful. I AM wonderful. I AM true. I AM honest. I AM magnificent. I AM glorious. I AM confident. I AM able to move all obstructions from my path. I AM capable and able. I AM civic. I AM intellect. I AM binary. I AM operational. I AM inspirational. I AM tough. I AM model of the universes. I AM quantum. I AM troubadour. I AM humble of the Earth. I AM philosopher. I AM scholar. I AM torch and bearer of Light and Love. I AM Light and Love in perfect human form. So it is uttered, so it is.

3. I AM Creator

There is nothing I cannot do. I AM provider. I can provide for self and any others that I wish or desire to. I AM obtainer. There is nothing I cannot obtain if I but wish or desire to. I AM shaper of myself. I AM able to cause myself to be that which I desire to be. I AM former of self. No one causes me to be save self. I AM captain of my own ship, which includes relationships. I AM captain of self. I AM dream maker. I AM able to take my dreams and desires and bring them into reality. I AM Creator. I Create. So it is uttered, so it is.

4. I AM Master

I AM image of God on Earth. I can master all that I desire. I AM able to acquire all information necessary for me to achieve anything. I AM a seeker. I AM a teacher. I AM great in and of myself. I AM not an island. I AM communal. I AM able to isolate from others when the need arises to collect myself, reflect upon my previous actions, behaviors, and decisions, and then reintroduce or reintegrate myself back into society at a higher vibration than I was previous to the self-imposed isolation. I AM fluent in speech and projection. I AM orator and professor to self and others. I AM Master and Master I shall be. So it is uttered, so it is.

5. I Am Disciple

I AM a disciple of life. I AM able to learn or remember from my mis-takes. I AM listener to all without judgment. I AM not prone to contempt prior to investigation as I was before. I AM a discerner of truth. I AM watcher. I AM able to observe and take in that which I need to improve myself. I AM open-minded. I AM capable of reading and writing. I AM able to voice my opinion without anger. I AM able to control my temper always. I AM capable of being passionate without being aggressive or submissive. I AM well-rounded and centered. I AM non-judgmental yet observational. I AM studious, able to pass all scholastic, professional or any other test placed before me by man to show my level of competency. I AM attentive to all. I AM remembering and growing in each given moment. So it is uttered, so it is.

6. I AM Energy

I AM body in motion. I AM able to do all the physical tasks necessary for self. I AM able to push away and out any restriction that may come upon or within my physical being, often with the assistance of my others. I AM able to send Light and Love outside of my being to my others, to places and spaces on Earth and beyond. I AM a most positive effect on the human stream of consciousness. I AM as healthy as I cause myself to be. I AM able to understand that I can heal myself. I AM atomic energy. I AM rejuvenating right now. I AM of healthy cells. I AM whole. I AM abundantly filled with power. I AM the energy of the universes. So it is uttered, so it is.

7. I AM Action

I AM able to get things done. I AM unstoppable. I AM unmovable when I must be yet movable when I need to be. I AM walking 10,000 steps each day on Earth. I AM sitting only when I need to rest, otherwise I AM moving. I AM a go-getter. I AM not to wait for opportunities to come to me; I AM going to them. I AM seeking truth at all times. I AM seeking the information that I need to improve self and assist others. I AM action propelled by self. So it is uttered, so it is.

8. I AM Self-sustaining

I AM able to take care of self. This includes my body, mind and spirit. I AM taking all of the supplements that I need to sustain self for my weight, height and skeletal frame. I AM reading daily high vibrational spiritual information. I AM sharpening my brain each and every day through games, puzzles and conversation. I AM acquiring the money I need to do the things that I need to do, go the places I need to go and assist the people I need to assist. I AM not a greedy person and anytime greed presents itself in my life I AM able and capable of turning away. I will turn away. So it is uttered, so it is.

9. I AM Gratitude

I AM grateful for all that I have, have had and will have. I AM grateful for my spouse or partner if that be the case. I AM grateful for my past spouse, spouses or partners if that be the case, which causes me to be open to the new spouse or partner that awaits me. I AM grateful for my parents. I AM grateful for my children and grandchildren if that be the case. I AM grateful for my sisters or brothers and their families if that be the case. I AM grateful for my friends. I AM grateful for my employment if that be the case. I AM grateful for the ability to pay all my bills. I AM grateful for all things. I AM grateful to be a messenger of Source/God. So it is uttered, so it is.

10. I AM Peace

I AM a peaceful spiritual warrior. I AM peaceful and loving. I AM at peace with all beings, all animals, all thoughts and ideas, even if I do not agree with such. I AM able to disengage from confrontation. I AM never looking for a fight, verbally or physically. I AM, however, to always protect myself and those in my bloodline if my or their life is at risk. I AM understanding that this is totally acceptable to Source/God and the universes. So it is uttered, so it is.

11. I AM Compassion

Compassion, I AM. I AM grace, the very virtue that comes to me from Source/God. I AM knowing full well that there is not sin or hell. Therefore, I AM grace through my acceptance of my others no matter what they have done, will do, might do, say, don't say, have said. I AM compassion for I know full well that each of us on Earth behaves as we do, or have, contingent upon the information that we have received and accepted at the vibration that we may be. I AM compassion for I let all that seek hear the aforementioned words from my very being. I pity myself and others when I or they make mis-takes. I AM, however, never to beat myself up for my decisions. So it is uttered, so it is.

12. I AM Humble

I AM humus of the Earth as all creatures on planet Earth are. I AM humble for even though I know there is nothing that I can't do, I AM also knowing I need assistance from my others to accomplish those things that I am not able to do on my own. I AM humble for I understand that I have gifts and others may possess some gifts that I do not. Therefore, sometimes I must seek outside myself. So it is uttered, so it is.

13. I AM Present

I AM present for I live in the here and now. I AM in the moment for the moment is all I have. I AM in full understanding that all time is the same; the past, present and future are one. I AM present because, through understanding the moment, I AM able to use the past to live in the present and thus positively affect the future. So it is uttered, so it is.

14. I AM Introspective

I AM introspective for I AM continually looking at myself. I AM introspective for each day I check myself, my thoughts, my actions. I AM introspective for I AM able to apologize to myself if I make mis-takes. I AM introspective for I AM able to apologize to others, even when my mental tells me I should or need not. I AM introspective for I am, when necessary, able to discard that which I need not anymore. I AM introspective for when I have done something to harm or hurt myself or my others, I AM able to remember that it was not of a high vibration and that it is not in my highest good to repeat such behaviors. So it is uttered, so it is.

15. I AM Freedom of Choice

I AM freedom of choice for I do that which I desire and wish to. I AM freedom of choice for I make my own decisions. I always have and always will. I AM freedom of choice for I fully understand that no one has ever and will ever make me do anything that I do not desire or wish to do even if, at the time, it is not in my highest good. I AM freedom of choice because by accepting such, I AM able to change, to grow, to evolve. So it is uttered, so it is.

16. I AM Hope

I AM hope for I have hope for myself, for my others, for the trees,

flowers, plants, animals, mankind as a whole, the mass consciousness, our planet, for the universes. I AM hope for I believe in miracles. I AM hope for I know things can change; all things change.
I AM hope for I have hope in Source/God. So it is uttered, so it is.

17. I AM Positive

I AM positive for I look at the bright side of all things. I AM positive
for when I look at the glass as half-empty, I AM able to change and
look at it as half-full. I AM positive for I see the God in all, even
those that may not be presenting such. I AM positive for I know
they can change as I have. I AM positive for I look to the positive
future of myself, my others and planet Earth. So it is uttered, so it is.

18. I AM Radiant

I AM radiant for all whom see my face and hear my voice shall
know that I AM assured of self. I AM always sending out a light
of joy from my very being. I AM shining, glowing in all directions
from my aura. So it is uttered, so it is.

19. I AM Love

I AM love. I was born in love; I will die in love. I AM love for I
can be nothing else. I AM caring, giving, protective, honest, true,
stable, grounded, centered, driving, and determined. I AM in the
image of Source/God which is love. Therefore, so Love I AM. So
it is uttered, so it is.

20. I AM Never Alone

I AM never alone for Source/God is with me, in me, through me, under me, over me, and all around me. I AM and have never been disconnected from Source/God. I AM connected to the highest vibration of all the Angels, Masters, Teachers, and Healers of past, present and future. I AM connected to all stars, galaxies and universes. I AM here. I AM there. I AM Everywhere and yet Nowhere, Now Here. I AM that which I AM. I can be nothing else. So it is uttered, so it is.

Let the Reader Read. Let the Hearer Hear! These are and shall always be the Discourses of I AM for mankind for your home, your planet, your Earth. Adhere to them and you and your world will change. Shout them to US, to self and others. Fore, they are the Keys to Ascension. You are on the path to Ascension—Continue. We Love You, Remember!

More Useful Decrees

I AM beautiful! I AM beautiful! I AM beautiful! And I AM ready for a wonderful day! I AM ready to give all that I can give and receive all that I can.

Mighty I AM Presence, do everything for me and through me perfectly. Remove all doubt from me. Help me to speak only the purest Truth in everything I say. Keep me humble in every way, positive to the world, and forever in the service of the Divine. And so it is uttered, so it is done.

I AM protected always, at all times, from all low-vibration entities and any negative energy directed towards me and the Light for which I stand. And so it is uttered, so it is done.

I AM refreshed, re-energized, renewed, rejuvenated, and healed in the healing power and the Light of the Christ every day in every way and at all times. And so it is uttered, so it is done.

I AM my Perfect Body. I AM Eternal Youth and Beauty. I AM an instrument of peace. And so it is uttered, so it is done.

I AM a perfect expression of perfect love here and now. I AM patient, kind, understanding, and respectful towards all those who do not understand or are unwilling to accept my beliefs. And so it is uttered, so it is done.

I AM making a positive difference in the lives of humanity. I AM helping humanity to awaken and expand their minds in a positive, loving way. And so it is uttered, so it is done.

I AM releasing NOW, with ease and grace, all that no longer serves me and my path so that I may fulfill my life's purpose here on Earth. And so it is uttered, so it is done.

Faith

Miracles are the norm for those with faith.
~ Source/God through Elliott Eli Jackson

A strong faith can overcome any fear. Faith is the substance of things hoped for and the evidence of things not yet seen. Faith is knowing; faith is believing. Faith is confidence in someone or something. Faith is trust in God and in the process of life. Faith does not question.

Faith allows us to grow. Faith is trusting in the outcome, no matter what it might be. Faith is comforting when facing serious problems or stressful situations. Faith is the evidence of things not seen. Faith is never giving up or losing sight of a goal.

Faith is to know we will always have what we need. Faith is

allowing life to unfold. Faith is victory. Faith is freedom. Faith is a virtue.

Through Faith, miracles happen!

Ho'oponopono

Ihaleakala Hew Len, Ph.D., was a master teacher who cured every patient in the criminally insane ward of a Hawaii State Hospital without ever seeing a single patient. He used an ancient Hawaiian practice known as Ho'oponopono.

Everyone in our life is an aspect of us. We all play roles for each other. For example, an addict you know may be reflecting what you may have been in the past (past lives included). When you work to heal this aspect of yourself, you help heal the addict.

Healing takes place through the repetition of four simple statements:

I'm sorry.

Please forgive me.

Thank you.

I love you.

Close your eyes. Picture the person that is a reflection of you in your mind, and then recite these four simple statements with sincerity. The more you recite them, the sooner the healing can take place.

Ho'opopono heals through loving one's self. This powerful healing process can "clear your mind of unconscious blocks to help you get what you truly want from life. It clears beliefs, thoughts, and memories from past lives that hold you back in your current life."

In addition, Dr. Len suggests filling a blue glass bottle with the purest water you can find. Set the bottle in the sunlight (preferably outside) for 10 to 60 minutes, or up to 12 hours for a stronger effect. This will charge the water with a healing blue light. If no sun is available, use incandescent lighting. Do not use LED or fluorescent lighting. Set your intention for the "blue water" to remove recurring memories or behavior patterns playing in the background, freeing you from their effects. [66]

Give it the test of time. Based on my own personal experience, Ho'oponopono really does work.

How to Recognize True Messengers

With the thinning of the veil, more and more people are able to channel information today, but it is important to note not all of the information channeled comes from high-vibrational beings (even if the person channeling claims it does). There are tricksters in the spirit realm, and if the person channeling the information is not of a high vibration, neither is their information.

"Be on guard against false prophets, who come to you in sheep's clothing but underneath are wolves on the prowl. You will know them by their deeds." (Matthew 7: 15-16)[67]

Discernment must be used to recognize the characteristics of a true messenger. To recognize a true messenger of the Divine as stated in *Man—His Origin, History and Destiny*:[68]

- Dictations are clear and concise, containing much substance, detail, and hard facts. Dictations that deal in generalities are not or a true messenger. Messages do not contain any "fluff" or amount of "feel good."

- A true messenger focuses how to gain personal ascension and how to bring in the next Golden Age. A true messenger will teach self-mastery.

- Is the motive of the channel to serve the Light or for personal and/or monetary gain? The key personality trait of a true messenger is true humility. Spiritual pride brought down Atlantis and Lemuria. If the channeled information feeds the ego of the channel even one crumb, it is not from the Divine. Beloved Master Kuthumi taught: "That which, even most subtly, stimulates the lower bodies and the soul to personal aggrandizement and inflation of the separate ego, is not of God."[69]

- A true messenger does not charge for channeled information. "Freely have you received; freely shall you give."[70] A reasonable fee is allowed to be charged for expenses for printing of books and brochures, travel for speaking engagements, etc. If someone charges a large amount for channeled information, that person is not of a high vibration. Greed has entered into the equation, and there is no place for greed when doing Lightwork.

- A true messenger does not assume any titles such as Master, Goddess, Guru, or Vicar of Christ. It is egoic; the messenger is not who he/she claims to be.

- In order to maintain a high vibration, the messenger needs to refrain from eating meat whenever possible. Eating meat can dull the senses.

- A true messenger must have a high state of spiritual

development and training (current or past lives). All channeled information must be available for all of mankind. The student must use discernment and test to make sure the information is of a high vibration. Information should not be accepted on faith alone. Question, question, question everything, again and again. Master Kuthumi: "Many false mediators have come, but you can always test their reality in this manner: If their teaching turns the outer self to the individual I AM Presence, that mediator comes from God. If such a teacher makes the individual dependent on his/her personal identity and keeps the aspirant looking to him or her for instruction and guidance, rather than his own divine source, then such a one is not a true mediator. To misrepresent the truth is not the will of God."[71]

- A true messenger does not make students dependent on him/her. If the information does not guide the student to look at him or herself or to go within for answers, the messenger is not of a high vibration. If the messenger teaches that one can become an angel, he or she is not of a high vibration. A spirit in human form can never be an angel.

- A true messenger will ask their students to raise their own vibration through decrees. A true messenger will ask their students to develop a healthy, strong physical body, the temple of the living God.

- Masters never threaten or use force. "A true messenger is always in full control of his faculties at all times. He can stop hearing the messages at will. There is no shaking of the physical form or "possession" that takes place when a channel is under the control of an entity."[72]

- A true channel knows he/she is responsible (karma) for any misrepresentation to the student. A true messenger gives credit where credit is due.
- A true messenger does not predict the date of a cataclysm or a great shift in mankind. There is no time on the Other Side. Time was created by man, for man.
- A true messenger can be recognized by the fruits of their labor. Their many accomplishments and miracles will be the result of their work.

"Adhering to the truth means change, change in attitude and behavior, even change in friends and your way of life. Most students resist change. The Masters said that the Goddess of Truth is not very popular with mankind. However, the Goddess of Love and Mercy are very popular. "[73] The Truth shall set you free.

When the student is ready, the teacher will come. There is no magic fairy wand that will take you into the New Age or keep you from being responsible for what you created.

Do not rely on just one channel or one book, for there is much information already published. You do not need to go from channel to channel to discover the latest truths.

Listen to Your Inner Guidance

It is important to know the difference between that which is your inner guidance and that which is not. Information is received in the same way—thought.

Your Ego

Ego is "Edging God Out." It is self-centered instead of other-centered. It works for the good of self, not for the good of all. It will either inflate you or deflate you, depending on how you feel and what you want to hear at the moment. Examples:

"Don't go out with that loser, or he'll ruin your reputation."

"That piece of apple pie is going straight to her thighs!"

Logic

Logic is the mental voice that uses past experience, statistics, probability, and reason to communicate with you. It is based on knowledge and facts. You draw on logic from your own and others' experiences. Examples:

"The last time you tried doing that you broke your ankle. Chances are you'll probably hurt it again."

"There's a traffic jam ahead. Reroute so you will get you there faster."

Spirit Guides

Your spirit guides know the bigger picture, while your ego lives in the moment. Their job is to keep you on track with your life plan. This sometimes means you may not like what they have to say. For instance, they might see the best way to teach you to value money is through bankruptcy. Examples:

"You'd be wise to accept the job in Los Angeles. It's what you've been waiting for your whole life."

"You know in your heart that he's not right for you."

Low Vibrations

Low vibrations work to keep you spirit down and take you off your spiritual path. They whisper negative thoughts in your ear that feed upon stored traumas and fears. They keep you in a state of fear. They incite prejudices and racism. They gain control over you through addiction. They can even try to get you to hurt or kill another. You believe what they have to say. You feel anxious and depressed because your vibration is low. Examples:

"Nobody loves you."

"You don't need to exercise today. So what if you miss a day! It won't hurt you."

"He doesn't love you so you might as well cheat on him."

Know your energy! Know when lower vibration entities are on you. Don't let them play you. Work to release them. Work to raise your vibration. Be the power plant so they will stay away.

Manifestation

Use the power of creative visualization to create positive changes in your life. It can help to achieve your goals and overcome limitations, and it can promote success in every aspect of your life.

Ten proven steps to manifest your desires include:[74]

1. **Motive:** What is the purpose of your desire? Is it for the very best and highest good for all concerned?
2. **Meditate:** Visualize a clear picture of the desired result and feel how happy you will be when it happens. Do not focus on how you will achieve this or you limit the Divine as to the possibilities of how it will take place. Hold that vision.

3. **Walk away:** Give yourself time to decide if this is what you really want. Revise your visualization, if necessary. Once you content with your desired visualization, do not make any changes. Create a vision board to help manifest your desire, using markers and magazine pictures.

4. **Decree:** "I AM the full manifestation of my heart's desire, and I ask my desire to be fulfilled." Say it out loud with meaning. Feel it in your heart. When you say the words, "I AM," you are calling on God, the Great I Am, to help bring your heart's desire into manifestation. Don't let obstacles deter you. Shift negative thoughts into positive thoughts. BELIEVE, knowing that all things are possible with God.

5. **Ask for help:** Ask the Source/God and all of the Divine to protect your vision and to energize it with their own feeling, mastery, and confidence. Give gratitude in advance for your desire already taking place. In return for their assistance, be in service in some way to help increase the Light of the world.

6. **Repeat:** Repeat this every day, preferably in the morning when your mind is clear.

7. **Maintain:** Maintain a sense of calm until your manifestation occurs.

8. **Do not share your vision with anyone:** Other people's negative thoughts ("They can't do it; that's impossible!") can affect the outcome. They may also be a reflection of your own self-doubt.

9. **Repeat:** Repeat your decree and give gratitude for the

help received every day until the manifestation occurs. Never give up!

10. **Journal:** Journal your experience. Journaling adds to the momentum needed to achieve success.

Prayer and Meditation

"Silence is essential. We need silence, just as much as we need air, just as much as plants need light. If our minds are crowded with words and thoughts, there is no space for us." ~ Thich Nhat Hanh

Prayer is speaking to God, and meditation is listening to God.

Prayer and meditation have a profound effect on our well-being. People who pray and meditate daily have lower stress levels, age less and live longer, and maintain a state of calm. They are better prepared to handle the trials and tribulations of life.

Ten minutes a day is better than one hour a week; 30 minutes a day is preferred. Make it a regular habit. Talk to God out loud; talk about anything and everything—what you like, what you don't like, what you want out of life. Exercise patience. Recognize when your prayer has been answered; give gratitude. Give gratitude for unanswered prayers. Unanswered prayers are quite often prayers that have been answered.

A regular practice of prayer and meditation will help you progress on your spiritual journey. It is a way to open and expand your mind, to stay in touch with your inner self, and to keep you from getting caught up in worldly ways; it will keep darkness away.

Through prayer and meditation you learn patience, releasing, hope, faith, trust, love, and true happiness. Your connection to God and all of the Divine strengthens each time you pray and meditate. You know that you are never really alone. You know that you are loved.

How to Pray

Most people pray over and over for the same thing. These repetitive prayers demonstrate a lack of faith in the person reciting the prayer.

The correct way to pray is to state your request, and then give gratitude in advance for what you would like. This shows you have faith and trust your request will be answered.

An analogy: A mother goes into the grocery store with her child. The child asks the mother for a candy bar, and the mother tells the child he can have one when she checks out if he is good while she shops.

The child goes through the store, whining and complaining, "Mommy, I want my candy bar. Mommy, I want it now. Mommy, when can I have my candy bar? Mommy, why can't I have it? I want it NOW, Mommy!" If you were the child's mother, wouldn't you want to take the child out of the store and go home?

A trusting child would go through the store saying, "Thank you for the candy bar I'm going to get, Mommy. I really appreciate it. It's going to taste really good. I'm going to love it. Thank you, Mommy. You're the best!" If you were the child's mother, wouldn't you want to hurry up shopping to give this child three candy bars?

Praying over and over for the same thing shows a lack faith. Instead pray for what you want, and then give gratitude in advance for what will take place, it shows you have faith. Gratitude is the highest form of prayer there is.

How to Meditate

Meditation begins when thinking ends. Mastering the technique of meditation takes much practice; it takes commitment. Meditation and reaching deeper spiritual states must be experienced. The amount of effort you put into your practice will determine the outcome.

Meditation has great health benefits. It can strengthen the immune system and lower blood pressure as the heart beats more slowly. Meditation helps foster a healthy mind to release negative mental states—fear, worry, and anger—and it can replace these emotions with positive attitudes. It can help to release stress, anxiety, and depression. It can help you to feel more relaxed, more peaceful, and more cheerful. Meditation can give you the ability to be more centered and more in control of yourself. As you can see, it can help to improve all areas of your life.

There are three stages to meditation: relax the body and mind, concentrate on the breath or an object, and expand your sense of being to realize you are in unity with all of creation.

Meditate daily with your eyes open for 10 minutes to align your bodies and to be at peace. Meditate once a week for 30 to 60 minutes with your eyes closed for a deeper connection to God.

The best time to meditate is in the morning when you first wake up, before eating. Set aside a place that is only used for meditation if you can to create a meditative mood and raise the vibration of the room. You can also mediate in nature.

A good way to meditate is to sit on a straight-backed chair. Sit slightly away from the back of the chair, keeping your spine erect (especially the lower spine) to avoid unnecessary pressure, and place your palms upright at the junction of the thighs and hips. Bring your shoulders back a bit to keep from slumping.

Begin and end your meditation with a prayer. Meditation helps align all your bodies so synchronicity can take place in your life. When energy is flowing through you, everything flows in life.

Answers to your prayers may show up in the words of a song, the words of another person, a sign on a truck or building, or in other ways. Be open to what life is showing you.

To Meditate with Your Eyes Open

Begin by taking three or four deep, cleansing breaths, in through the nose and out through the mouth. Relax your body, then focus on something inside or outside the room that moves. This can be a flag or tree blowing, the flicker of a candle flame, or a rotating ceiling fan. The movement of the object will help move the thoughts from your mind. Spend 10 minutes in meditation and your day will flow smoothly. You will sleep better, and you will be more at peace throughout the day.

Raising Your Vibration

Prayer and meditation, music and beauty are tools typically used to raise your vibration, but then reality settles in and our vibration goes right back to where it once was. To raise your vibration more permanently, release the many traumas and fears held in your energy field.

Our energy field holds all of our memories, fears, and traumas from current and past lives. Imagine this energy field dotted with tiny pixels, black or white in color. Black pixels represent traumas and fears, while white pixels represent pleasant, happier times and love. From a distance, our energy field looks gray. The darker the gray, the more fearful we are. The lighter the gray, the more of love we become.

Most of us have energy fields that are 51 percent or more gray. In other words, we have more fears and traumas stored than we could ever imagine! Fear is the result of a trauma. Heal the trauma that created the fear, and then work to overcome the fear.

Heal the past to heal the present. The more healing that takes place, the softer, more peaceful, and more loving we become.

Relationships

People come and go in our life. Some were only meant to be in our life for a short period of time. They provide some purpose, but soon fade away.

Some people are amazing in the beginning, but they take more than they are willing to give. They offer little help and support, especially during challenging times, and eventually fade away.

And then there are people who stay with you for a long time, especially when things get tough. We depend on them through good times and bad. And with time, even these people fade away. Sometimes they come back, and the relationship gets stronger.

People come and go in our life just as we come and go in the lives of others. For every ending, there is a new beginning. We grow together and we grow apart. This is the cycle of life.

There are times when we are left standing, feeling alone, like nobody cares. And then along comes someone else who is just like us, and we're on to a new beginning. We were never meant to be alone. If we are, it is by choice (consciously or unconsciously).

As long as we are in a relationship, we are getting something out of it, such as love, support, attention, or money. When the relationship is no longer fed, one person departs, leaving the other to feel abandoned and betrayed because we didn't see it coming. The signs are always there if you look.

Not everyone you lose in life is a loss. You shared gifts and received blessings. Move on. They were not meant to be permanent.

Don't let anyone hold you back. Allow yourself to grow. Don't be held back by someone who isn't ready to grow.

It is through the challenging times that relationships grow stronger or fall apart. A true friend can't make our problems disappear, but they won't disappear when times get tough. Recognize true friends as you open yourself up to deeper, more meaningful relationships.

Treasure the friends who care, and release those who no longer serve you. Accept the roles we play for each other. Look for the blessing in every relationship.

Release Letters

You can't change what happened, but you can change how you feel about what happened. Releasing someone heals all wounds. True release comes from the heart. It frees the soul to move on. Words are easily spoken, but not always meant.

Apologize for whatever you may have contributed to the

situation, intentionally or unintentionally, and release whomever may have hurt you. And don't forget to apologize to yourself for your lack of understanding. If you are the victim, you were probably the perpetrator at some point in time. You may be getting back something you once gave out (karma).

Apologize for not accepting others for who they are, and release yourself for not accepting yourself for who you are.

Many people pray to God for forgiveness because it is much easier to ask God than to face the person we hurt. Apologize to the person hurt. You do not need God's forgiveness for, in Truth, you have never done anything wrong—only experienced! God knows both parties are learning lessons through their experiences. It is important to apologize to the person you hurt. Accept responsibility for your mistake and work to heal the situation. If the person you need to apologize to has crossed over, write a release letter to them. It will benefit both of you.

Releasing is a requirement if true and lasting change is desired.

Release Letter to Someone Else
Do this for others first, then for the self–you will be amazed at how powerful this letter really is!

Write a letter to whomever you need to release or to whom you must apologize; be sincere. If the letter is not written from the heart, nothing will change. Do not write the letter if you still hold a grudge against someone. Your intention must be pure.

This is a wonderful tool to release old emotions (current and past lives). Write anything you would like to say. You can even swear. The important thing is to get "stuck" negative thoughts and emotions out so you can be at peace. For example, you can say: "You hurt me when…" "Why did you do that? What were you trying to prove?" "How could you do that to me? You really hurt me." "That was dumb! What were you thinking?!"

Release this person who has hurt you, intentionally or unintentionally, all the way back to the root where the problem began (this is very important). Heal the past to heal the present. When looking at the weed on top of the ground (current life), you do not see the roots hidden beneath the ground (past lives).

Apologize for anything you may have done to hurt this person, intentionally or unintentionally, in your many lifetimes together (current and past). Most likely, you both have contributed to the problem in one lifetime or another, and that is why you are together now. Unresolved issues keep us tied together throughout eternity until they are resolved.

Send love to this person—all the way back to the root life. At the end of the letter, include this statement:

"I love you very much, and I release you. I apologize for not accepting you exactly as you are."

Take your letter to a place that is sacred to you and to God, and then read it out loud.

Tear the letter up, then burn it. Make sure every last piece of paper is burnt (symbolic of purification). You don't want to leave anything behind.

Now take the ashes outside and say:

"Dear God, this has been a burden I no longer wish to carry. Please resolve it for me in the Divine White Light of the Holy Spirit. Gratitude."

Toss the ashes into the wind.

Visualize an etheric cord that binds the two of you together by removing it from you first, then the other person. This cord can usually be found at the solar plexus, although it can be anywhere. Place the cord into the Platinum Flame. You will feel different!

Release Letter to Yourself

Write a letter to yourself, writing from the heart. This is a wonderful tool to release old stuck emotions (current and past lives). Write anything you would like to say to yourself. You can even swear, if so desired. The important thing is to get "stuck" negative thoughts and emotions out so you can be at peace. When you have peace within, there is peace in your world.

In the letter, you can say anything you want. For example, you can ask yourself: "Why did you say/do that?" "That was dumb! What were you thinking?!" "Why did you make that decision about that job?" "Why do you keep falling into the same old trap?"

Be sure to address any fears you may have that you are ready to release, anything you don't like about yourself, and any problems you may have with someone else (they are a mirror back to you).

Release yourself for whatever you feel you may have done wrong (for being too judgmental or critical of yourself, for doubting yourself, for not loving yourself, etc.).

Release yourself for not accepting you for who you really are—a work in progress. (We strive for perfection, but we are not there yet!)

And be sure to send love to yourself.

At the end of the letter, include this statement:

"I love you very much, and I release you. I apologize for not accepting you exactly as you are."

Take your letter to a place that is sacred to you and to God, and then read it out loud.

Tear the letter up, then burn it. Make sure every last piece of paper is burnt (symbolic of purification). You don't want to leave anything behind.

Then look in the mirror into your eyes (the eyes are the entrance way to the soul) and say:

"I release you, and I love you very much."

Now take the ashes outside and say:

"Dear God, this has been a burden I no longer wish to carry. Please resolve it for me in the Divine White Light of the Holy Spirit. Gratitude."

Toss the ashes into the wind. You will feel different!

Trust and Surrender

Just when you think nothing is going to happen,
something will happen. So don't give up!
~ Source/God through Elliott Eli Jackson

We have been learning life lessons through experience. Trust and surrender are required in order to release fear. Trust in the process of life, and surrender to the outcome. Let go and let God!

When you surrender yourself to God, the universe will provide all the situations and opportunities needed to balance all your issues and bring about healing. When you surrender to the process with absolute faith and trust, without judgment or fear, you can get through any situation with ease and grace.

Old negative behavioral patterns and belief systems that block love must be released. When we surrender to God, it will no longer matter what other people think of us. We will begin to follow our own truth and listen to our own heart.

The first step is the hardest and most overwhelming. As Lao-Tzu taught, the journey of a thousand miles begins with the first step. The first step is always the hardest. Trust that once you have taken the first step, the rest will be much easier. The more you practice this, the more you will succeed.

Endnotes

1   https://www.phrases.org.uk/bulletin_board/5/messages/1614.html

2   *The New American Bible,* © 1971 Catholic Publishers, Inc., All rights reserved.

3   https://www.goodreads.com/quotes/1339572-when-the-student-is-ready-the-teacher-will-appear-when

4   *The Sapiential Discourses: Universal Wisdom Book* III, by All There Is Was and Ever Shall Be through Elliott Eli Jackson, © 2017 Independently published, All rights reserved.

5   https://www.space.com/24854-how-old-is-earth.html

6   https://www.bbc.com/news/science-environment-31718336

7   *The New American Bible,* © 1971 Catholic Publishers, Inc., All rights reserved.

8   *Man—His Origin, History and Destiny*, compiled by Werner Schroeder, © 1984 Ascended Master Teaching Foundation.

9   *The New American Bible,* © 1971 Catholic Publishers, Inc., All rights reserved.

10 *Man—His Origin, History and Destiny*, compiled by Werner Schroeder, © 1984 Ascended Master Teaching Foundation.

11 Ibid.

12 http://www.ntd.tv/2017/01/08/6-evil-dictators-notorious-mass-killings-modern-history/

13 http://www.newworldencyclopedia.org/entry/Gehenna

14 https://www.catholic.com/qa/did-sheol-become-gehenna-after-the-resurrection

15 https://www.merriam-webster.com/dictionary/lord

16 https://en.wikipedia.org/wiki/Swastika

17 http://wordcentral.com/cgi-bin/student?book=Student&va=bible+

18 https://www.biblica.com/resources/bible-faqs/when-was-the-bible-written

19 https://www.npr.org/templates/story/story.php?storyId=124572693

20 https://www.britannica.com/event/Council-of-Nicaea-Christianity-325

21 https://www.britannica.com/biography/Constantine-I-Roman-emperor

22 https://www.pbs.org/wgbh/pages/frontline/shows/religion/story/emergence.html

23 https://www.huffingtonpost.com/bernard-starr/why-christians-were-denied-access-to-their-bible-for-1000-years_b_3303545.html

24 Ibid.

25 Ibid.

26 http://time.com/4821911/king-james-bible-history

27 https://www.britannica.com/topic/King-James-Version

28 Ibid.

29 http://gnosis.org/naghamm/nhl.html

30 *The Sapiential Discourses: Universal Wisdom Book* II, by All There Is Was and Ever Shall Be through Elliott Eli Jackson, © 2014 Independently published, All rights reserved.

31 *The Sapiential Discourses: Universal Wisdom Book* III, by All There Is Was and Ever Shall Be through Elliott Eli Jackson, © 2017 Independently published, All rights reserved.

32 Ibid.

33 https://www.near-death.com/paranormal/edgar-cayce/human-origins.html

34 https://churchleaders.com/pastors/pastor-articles/139575-7-startling-facts-an-up-close-look-at-church-attendance-in-america.html

35 https://www.poets.org/poetsorg/poem/you-it-act-ii-scene-vii-all-worlds-stage

36 *The Sapiential Discourses: Universal Wisdom Book* III, by All There Is Was and Ever Shall Be through Elliott Eli Jackson, © 2017 Independently published, All rights reserved.

37 *The Sapiential Discourses: Universal Wisdom Book* III, by All There Is Was and Ever Shall Be through Elliott Eli Jackson, © 2017 Independently published, All rights reserved.

38 Ibid.

39 Ibid.

40 *The Seven Sacred Flames*, by Aurelia Louise Jones © 2007 by Mount Shasta Light Publishing. All rights reserved.

41 https://www.cbsnews.com/news/do-antidepressants-cause-depression-what-new-study-says

42 https://www.matthewbooks.com/june-18-2018/

43 https://www.ncbi.nlm.nih.gov/pmc/articles/PMC2077351/

44 https://www.healthline.com/health/healthy-sleep/foods-that-could-boost-your-serotonin

45 https://www.psychologytoday.com/us/conditions/dissociative-identity-disorder-multiple-personality-disorder

46 *Teachings for the New Golden Age ~ Kuthumi*, Ascended Master Teaching Foundation

47 *The New American Bible,* © 1971 Catholic Publishers, Inc., All rights reserved.

48 https://www.goodreads.com/quotes/7753246-a-woman-s-highest-calling-is-to-lead-a-man-to

49 http://www.quotationspage.com/quote/40272.html

50 https://www.goodreads.com/quotes/24499-be-the-change-that-you-wish-to-see-in-the

51 *The New American Bible,* © 1971 Catholic Publishers, Inc., All rights reserved.

52 https://www.goodreads.com/quotes/6946-not-all-of-us-can-do-great-things-but-we

53 http://www.thebestofrawfood.com/ph-test-strips.html

54 https://www.healthline.com/health/healthy-sleep/foods-that-could-boost-your-serotonin

55 https://blog.thatcleanlife.com/5-foods-that-fight-symptoms-of-depression/

56 https://universityhealthnews.com/daily/depression/8-natural-dopamine-boosters-to-overcome-depression/

57 *Modern Essentials,* @ 2016 Aroma Tools™. All rights reserved.

58 http://www.ams.usda.gov/AMSv1.0/ams.fetchTemplateData.do?template= TemplateN&leftNav=NationalOrganicProgram&page=NOPGoingOrganic& description=Going%2520Organic

59 http://www.aarp.org/food/healthy-eating/info-04-2012/real-organic-food.html

60 http://www.natural-health-well.com/how-do-essential-oils-work

61 http://www.cdc.gov/healthyweight/physical_activity/index.html

62 *The Sapiential Discourses: Universal Wisdom*, by All There Is Was and Ever Shall Be through Elliott Eli Jackson, © 2012 Independently published, All rights reserved.

63 https://sciencing.com/what-functions-umbilical-cord-4672809.html

64 *The Ascension Flame of Purification and Immortality* by Aurelia Louise Jones, © 2017 by Aurelia Louise Jones, Mt. Shasta Light Publishing, Mount Shasta, CA.

65 *The Sapiential Discourses: Universal Wisdom Book* III, by All There Is Was and Ever Shall Be through Elliott Eli Jackson, © 2017 Independently published, All rights reserved.

66 https://bluebottlelove.com/hew-len-hooponopono/

67 *The New American Bible,* © 1971 Catholic Publishers, Inc., All rights reserved.

68 *Man—His Origin, History and Destiny,* © 1984 Ascended Master Teaching Foundation, Mount Shasta, CA. All rights reserved.

69 *Man—His Origin, History and Destiny,* © 1984 Ascended Master Teaching Foundation, Mount Shasta, CA. All rights reserved.

70 Ibid.

71 Ibid.

72 Ibid.

73 Ibid.

74 *The Law of Precipitation: How to Successfully Meet Life's Daily Needs* by Werner Schroeder, © 2000 Ascended Master Teaching Foundation, Mount Shasta, CA.

White Dove Circle of Light and Love

is a unique, one-of-a-kind wellness center where one can
find true healing for the mind, body, and spirit.

Everyone has his or her own unique and different issues to heal,
and because our issues differ, no two people heal in the same way.

White Dove Circle is a leader in the holistic field offering a
wide variety of services and products to heal naturally.

Step into our beautiful wellness center and you immediately
feel a sense of calm; a sense of peace. You know that
where you are...is where you're supposed to be!

Come share your heart with us!

White Dove Circle of Light and Love
205 East Street
Springboro, OH 45066
937.806.3231
info@whitedovecircle.com
whitedovecircle.org

We are the Community of White Dove

SERVICE to Creator/God, to all of the Divine, and to all of our fellow man through:

> **Compassion**—understanding what others are going through, sharing our love with them
>
> **Mercy**—lending a helping hand to those who need it the most
>
> **Joy**—finding joy in everyone and everything in life; helping others find their joy

PEACE—inner and outer peace through:

> **Humility**—recognizing we are all one and that no one is better than another
>
> **Purity**—in our thoughts, words, actions, and deeds; in the way we live our life
>
> **Devotion**—having a strong connection with Creator/God and all of the Divine through prayer and meditation

RELEASING—of self and others through:

> **Faith**—in Creator/God and all of the Divine, knowing everything happens for a reason and a purpose
>
> **Hope**—for a better relationship with one's self and with others, doing our part to create a better world
>
> **Trust**—that through releasing we will find a much deeper love—unconditional love

TRUTH—the purest truth there is, standing strong in this truth through:

    Sincerity—in all we say and all we do, always working from a place of love

    Loyalty—to Creator/God and all of the Divine, to one's self (to thine own self be true)

    Courage—to speak our truth and to stand in our truth even when others do not understand

LIGHT AND LOVE—the foundation on which we are built

    Loving with all our hearts and all our souls, all of life and all of creation

    Spreading our light wherever we go to light the way for others to follow

    Sharing the Wisdom of the Masters with those who seek the Truth

Come share your heart with us!

www.ingramcontent.com/pod-product-compliance
Lightning Source LLC
Chambersburg PA
CBHW051950090426
42741CB00008B/1335